WAYS TO AMUSE
A CHILD

COOLGREANY,
CASTLEWARREN,
CO. KILKENNY.
TEL. NO. (0503) 26148

In the same series
Children's Party and Games Book
Uniform with this book

555 WAYS TO AMUSE A CHILD

Crafts, Hobbies and
Creative Ideas for the
Child from Six to Twelve

JUNE JOHNSON
Drawings by Beryl Bennett

PAPERFRONTS
**ELLIOT RIGHT WAY BOOKS
KINGSWOOD SURREY UK**

Copyright Notice
Originally published in the U.S.A. as 838 Ways to Amuse a Child
© June Johnson MCMLX.
U.K. edition abridged and adapted by arrangement with June Johnson
© Elliot Right Way Books MCMLXXXI.
This edition is not for sale in the U.S.A.

All rights reserved. No part of this book may be reproduced, stored in a retrieval system, or transmitted, in any form or by any means, electronic, photocopying, mechanical, recording or otherwise, without the prior permission of the copyright owner.

Conditions of sale
This book shall only be sold, lent or hired for profit, trade, or otherwise in its original binding, except where special permission has been granted by the Publishers.

Every effort is made to ensure that Paperfronts and Right Way Books are accurate, and that the information given in them is correct. However, information can become out of date, and author's or printer's errors can creep in. This book is sold, therefore, on the condition that neither Author nor Publisher can be held legally responsible for the consequences of any error or omission there may be.

Made and Printed in Great Britain by Love and Malcomson Ltd., Redhill, Surrey.

*To Phil
for 555 reasons*

CONTENTS

Introduction   9

1   Crafts   11

General Suggestions 11   Practical Aids 13   Modelling and Sculpturing 15   Designs: Paper and Paste, Crayon and Paint 20   Decorations and Accessories 29   Gifts to Give 47   Houses 53   Dolls 70   Toys of Paper and Paste 73

2   Hobbies   87

Ways to Build up a Hobby 87   Aeroplanes and Jets 89   Art 89   Braiding 90   Cars and Trucks 91   Coins 91   Cooking 92   Dolls 92   Flower Arranging 92   Gardening 94   Geography 96   History and Archaeology 96   Home Decorating 97   Knot Tying 97   Leatherwork 98   Pets 98   Photography 98   Prehistoric Times 99   Sewing 99   Ships 107   Stamps 107   Trains 108   Weaving 108   Whittling 110   Writing 111

3   Fun with Science   112

How to Be a Scientist 112   Astronomy 112   The Body 115   Chemistry 120   Crime Detection 121   Foods 122   Geography 123   Geology 124   Perspective 124   Physics 126   Soil Conservation 127   Weather 128

4 Nature Lore   131

Nature Hobbies: Animals 131 Aquarium 132 Birds 132 Flowers 134 Insects 134 Rocks 135 The Sea and Shells 136 Trees 137 Wild Pets 140 Nature Crafts 141 Hikes and Field Trips 147

5 Convalescence   152

Practical Hints 152 Play Ideas 155

6 Travel   162

What to Take 162 What to Bring Back 163 What to See 163 Games to Play in the Car 164 Excursions 168 Camping 169

Index   171

INTRODUCTION

MUST I AMUSE MY CHILD?

You picked up this book because the title attracted you. *Hundreds* of ways to amuse a child. Imagine! Convalescence and travel, nature and science, crafts and hobbies — a long list, and how wonderful for Bob and Mary.

Now, perhaps, as you stand with the book in your hand, second, more serious thoughts assail you. "Have I the obligation to amuse my children?" you wonder. "Have I, really, even the right? If they don't learn to amuse themselves, to live their own lives, in these years from six to twelve — when do they?"

You are quite right. You do not have the obligation to provide amusement for your children — not most of the time, as a matter of policy. And your children do indeed have the right, the wonderfully important right, to amuse themselves. This book seeks only to spread before them the vast panorama of a child's world, for their own choice, at their own time, in their own individual way.

A NOTE ON THE BOOK

555 Ways to Amuse a Child has been written primarily for simple home play. In most cases, the suggestions do not depend on elaborate materials or tools or parental skills. An effort was made to avoid the type of book where the parent says as he reads, "This would be wonderful *if* I had the time . . . *or* we owned those tools . . . or I knew how to . . . (read music, handle a jig saw, interpret scientific jargon)."

Young people, however, do need the tools of youth. They need balls and games and toys of all varieties. They need the supplies that make creative activities possible (these supplies are listed in Chapter 1 under "General Suggestions"). And certainly they need the books and records that mean so much to the growth of the inner youth. Fortunate the young people who grow up in a family that has the happy custom of giving books and records at each birthday and at Christmas.

So many excellent juvenile books are published today that no list could be complete. Most good bookshops and libraries have a large and varied children's selection.

1
CRAFTS

Families with school-age children often know the formulas and methods employed in the basic crafts. They are, therefore, not repeated in this book. However, a number of suggestions are listed below to assure success with the various crafts discussed in this chapter:

GENERAL SUGGESTIONS

1. Always begin a craft plan by first reading the entire instructions, to be sure all necessary materials are on hand, and to form a general picture of what is to be done.

2. If heavy paper or cardboard is to be folded, lay a ruler on the fold line, run a blunt knife such as a table knife along this edge, then fold.

3. Rubber cement and white glues are among the best all-round adhesives for paper and cloth. Where taping is suggested plastic tape is superior to Sellotape if the object is to be kept for any length of time. It comes in both a natural tone and colours.
   To set glue or paste on flat surfaces, place in a book under a weight or other books. The book can be protected by putting paper over and under the pasted item.

4. To cut circles if no compass is available, use bottoms of glasses, cups, etc., or plates turned upside-down.

5. For large sheets of paper, use wide shelf paper or cut open a giant paper bag. Glue several together if necessary.

6. "Craft" paper, also known as construction or art paper, is the term used in this book to describe the heavy sheets of many colours found in stationery stores.

7. Fine quality paste board is excellent for paper furniture, cards, etc., and can be found in art or stationery shops. Velvety paper, also in such shops, is expensive but can be used sparingly for frames, cards, etc.

8. Keep a box or drawer for craft supplies: paper rolls, boxes and cardboard of all types, corrugated wrapping paper. Other supplies to build up over a period of time:

FOR CRAFTS: Plaster of Paris, white glue, poster paints and brushes, clay, coloured craft paper, a sheet of velvety paper, crepe paper, newsprint, plastic tape, masking tape, various colours of enamel in small sizes; fine picture-hanging wire, leather punch, spray cans of varnish or shellac, coloured Sellotape, sequins, small beads, glitter, polystyrene, buttons, scraps of felt, lace, ribbon. Use oilcloth or plastic to protect work surfaces.

FOR THE DESK: Writing board, Sellotape, rubber bands, brass paper fasteners, paper clips, erasers of all kinds, crayons, scissors, ball-point pens and pencils (colours and black), large notebook, small pocket notebooks, notebook paper (lined for easier writing), gummed reinforcements, pencil sharpener, ruler, stapler, paper punch, India ink.

FOR SEWING: A sewing box (or make one), sets of pins and rather large needles, small boxes for embroidery thread, thimble, basic colours of thread, scissors, yarn bits, buttons, cloth measuring tape, darning egg or stool, all kinds of leftover scraps and materials.

FOR CARPENTRY: Not too heavy, but real rather than toy: hammer, small saw, screwdriver, pliers, steel measuring tape, square, vice, boxes or jars of nails, screws, and bolts in various sizes.

FOR REPAIRS: Household cement, plastic tape, plastic cement, glue.

PRACTICAL AIDS

Razor for Craft Use

Any kind of razor blade is dangerous for children but one could be used by the older child *under supervision*. Single-sided is best but difficult to obtain. A double-sided one can be made safer by winding adhesive tape around both ends with many thicknesses of tape over one edge to prevent cutting the fingers, leaving one sharp edge exposed. Or cheap plastic blade-holders can be obtained.

Reference File

To make a file for references and other purposes, get a small carton, about 13 inches wide, at the supermarket (Fig. 1, A). Buy inexpensive manila folders, or make some of two sheets of cardboard or craft paper taped together along one side. If you make your own, make a tab that stands above the folder (Fig. 1, B), to label the contents (such as "My Stories", "Fourth Form Spelling Tests", "Patterns", "Space News").

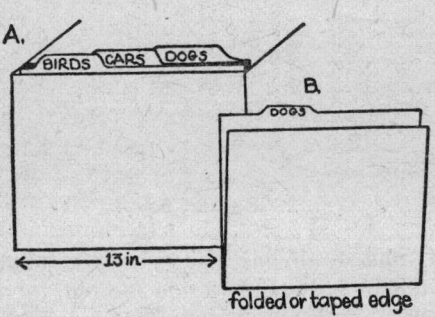

Fig. 1. (A) Reference file.
(B) Individual folder for file.

File the folders alphabetically ("*B*irds", "*D*oll Pictures", "*L*etters"). Until the box contains enough folders to remain upright, place a brick or stick in the box behind the folders.

When you find a pretty design, drop it into "Patterns", to copy at a future date. Letters to answer will be on hand under "Letters". Snapshots or scrapbook pictures that have not yet been placed in a book will not get lost. You will find dozens of uses for a file.

Booklet Boxes

If you do not have a file, booklets magazines or completed school exercise books may become lost or get torn. Even with a file they sometimes become too bulky. For such materials, make a book box.

Cut two pieces of cardboard slightly larger than the largest booklet or magazine. Cut a 3-inch-wide top, bottom, and two sides, as shown (Fig. 2). Use masking tape to tape the sides to the top, bottom and back.

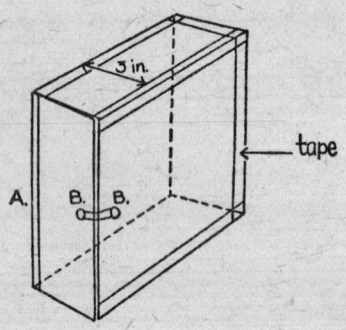

Fig. 2. Booklet box.

Tape the front down one side only (A), for a hinged door. Tape this one edge both inside and out, for strength.

Coat the entire outside surface of the box with glue or paste, one side at a time, and then cover with wallpaper scraps, wrapping paper, craft paper, or pieces of fabric. When thoroughly dry, fasten a brass paper-clasp handle, or sew a button to the opening flap, and another around the corner on the side of the box (B). Hold fastener with a rubber band, or a ribbon.

Fill with booklets or other materials and place on the book shelves.

MODELLING AND SCULPTURING

Plaster of Paris

Estimate the amount of plaster needed, and pour that amount of water into a clean food can. Slowly pour powder into the water without stirring, until a small peak forms above the water. This is enough of the powder. Then stir, keeping the spoon under the mixture to prevent air bubbles, which weaken it. Stir until the spoon leaves marks in the mixture, and then pour immediately. To slow setting, add a bit of vinegar; to speed setting, add pinch of salt.

Wash hands outdoors, and dispose of any leftover mixture there also to prevent clogging the drains.

Papier-Mâché

Prepare a large bowl full of one-inch squares of newspaper as follows: Tear off long inch-wide strips, holding as many strips as you can easily tear through, then tear these off by the inch. Completely cover the scraps with hot water and soak overnight.

Next, squeeze out excess water. Add one cup of paste to every three cups of paper and mix thoroughly. For paste, use the proportion of one third cup flour to one quarter cup of water. To avoid a messy mixing job, you may place in a plastic bag and knead.

Clay

Dry clay and glues for the following articles can be purchased in art or stationery stores. Follow package directions. Add glue to harden clay permanently without kiln drying.

BOWLS:

1. **Moulded bowl.** Hold a ball of clay in the left hand, or place on a work surface, in this case being careful not to stick it fast to the surface. Press with your thumb to make a hole in the centre, and with your fingers on the outside guide the shape (Fig. 3, A). Continue pressing and shaping,

turning it as you work, being careful to maintain the same thickness all the way around. The clay can be moulded into a round or oval shape, a shell or free form.

2. **Coil bowl.** Make long rolls of clay about the thickness of a large crayon or fountain pen. Coil this round and round, curving it in the shape desired. When finished this can be left as it is, with coils showing (Fig. 3, B), or the coils can be smoothed into a solid surface.

Candleholder: Make a round ball of clay and press a candle into the centre. Carefully remove candle and permit clay to harden (Fig. 3, C). Or shape the clay with the fingers,

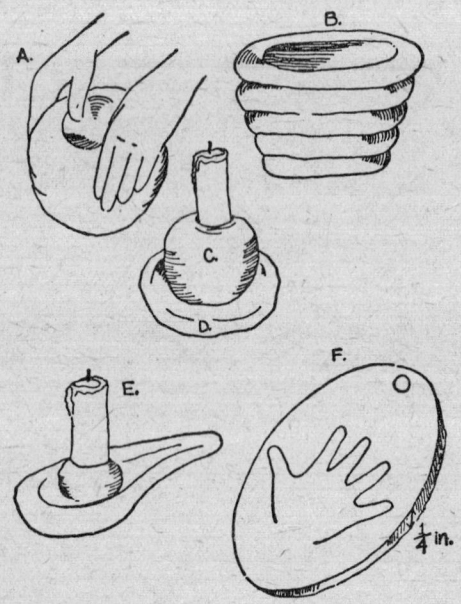

Fig. 3. Clay modelling.

(A) Moulded bowl.
(B) Coil bowl.
(C and D) Candle-holder with drip tray.
(E) Free-form candle-holder.
(F) Handprint.

Crafts

making a rim around the bottom to catch dripping wax (Fig. 3, D). Or make a free-form base, following any shape you choose (Fig. 3, E). Paint with poster paint or enamel when dry.

Handprint: Roll out a piece of clay ¼-inch thick and a bit larger than your hand. Place a plate over this and outline a circle, or make it slightly oval. Cut the edge with a knife or a straightened paper clip, smooth the edge with a finger, and then press the hand into the clay. While still damp use a pencil to make a hole for a hanging ribbon (Fig. 3, F). Paint with enamel when thoroughly dry.

Soap Carving

Use a soft, large cake of soap. Leave unwrapped for twenty-four hours to dry. Create a design on paper first, something simple, without too many angles or curves.

To carve, use a paring knife, not too sharp. Work over paper or a tray to catch carvings for household use later. First slice away brand name and raised edges, as little as

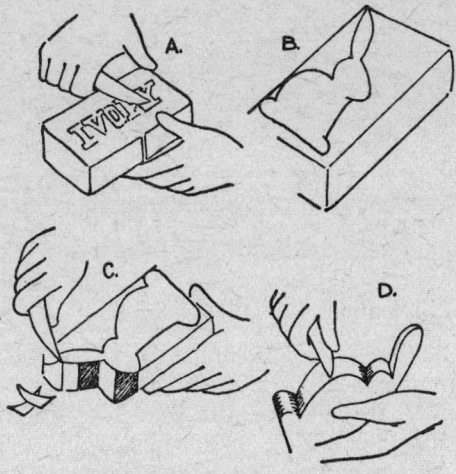

Fig. 4. Soap carving.

possible (Fig. 4, A). Trace the outline on the soap (B). Lay the soap on a breadboard or other surface for the first cutting and cut from top to bottom, removing excess soap (C).

For the general shaping of the piece, hold in the hand and carve as in peeling a potato. Work all around the design instead of doing one section, such as the head, first (D). Work from the high points that stand out to the low points, deeper in.

For finishing, smooth with the knife. Mark details such as eyes with an orange wood stick or sharpened wooden lollipop stick. Let set for a day or so to dry, then smooth *gently,* with face tissue, fingers and palm of hand.

Cotton Modelling (Animals)

For this, pure white surgical cotton can be used, or cheaper cotton wool. Cut off a piece about 6 inches square and roll from one corner diagonally to another, to make an oval ball. Paste the end down to prevent unrolling (Fig. 5).

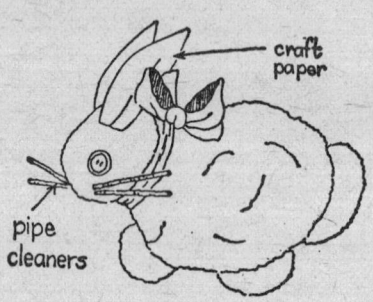

Fig. 5. Cotton modelling.

About one-third of the distance from the end, tie a pretty bow to form the neck of the animal and separate the head from the body. Shape a face with your fingers. Use bits of felt, paper or other stiff material for ears and tongue, or even eyes, or use buttons, beads or sequins for eyes, and paste on. Add a small bell to the ribbon if desired.

Crafts 19

For legs and tail, shape bits of cotton and paste into place.

Sponge Animals

Cut pieces of sponge into the parts of the bodies of animals and cement together (Fig. 6).

Fig. 6 Sponge animal.

Box Designs

Put aside every pretty, odd or interesting small box you find. Add leftover paper towel tubes, used gift-wrapping

Fig. 7. Box design.

paper, scraps of cloth, and trimmings such as borders or lace. Collect pretty pins and buttons, beads, sequins, bits of bright felt, feathers.

Make animals, men, or abstract creatures from the boxes, and decorate with the other materials (Fig. 7).

DESIGNS: PAPER AND PASTE, CRAYON AND PAINT

Stencils

A stencil is a design cut within a solid, unbroken frame, to be transferred to another surface.

Make stencil designs on heavy paper or card (see Fig. 8). The pear, shown, is the cutout area. Very carefully hold or pin the stencil to the paper or material to be decorated. Use poster or textile paints and fill in the cutout area completely on the paper or cloth background. Paint with a small brush, always working from the edge of the stencil to the open centre of each design.

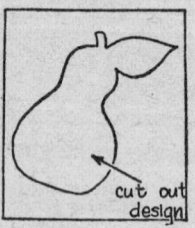

Fig. 8. Stencil.

To cut a stencil, use a Stanley knife or make a craft razor (see page 13). Patterns may be fruits flowers, vegetables, toys, etc. For a snowflake stencil, see Fig. 11.

Border Prints (Repeating Designs)

These can be used for putting an attractive border on the top and bottom of a knitting bag. They can be used to form a border for a scrapbook, or to frame a picture, or to decorate dolls' houses.

To make, cut a strip of gummed crêpe paper or craft paper exactly as wide and long as needed. Fold into half (Fig. 9, A), then into thirds (B). Draw any design you wish (C), and cut, remembering only that *some part of each edge must remain uncut*, or the designs will fall apart when unfolded (D). The pattern may be geometric, dolls, trees, flowers, birds, boats, etc.

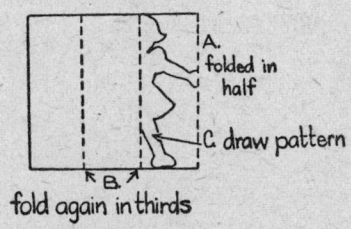

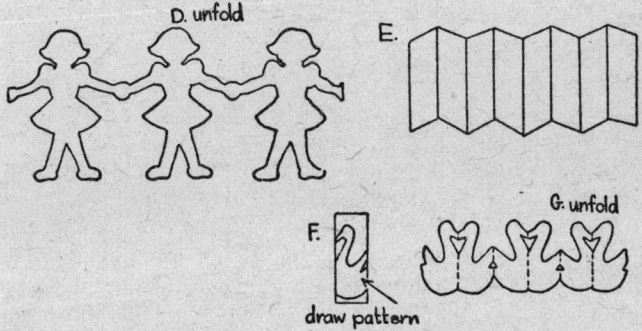

Fig. 9. Border prints.

(A-D) Single repeating design.
(E-G) Double repeating design.

To make double designs, facing each other, fold the long strip of paper accordion-style (E), in the size desired. Draw a pattern on the top fold (F), being sure edges of the design touch each side, cut, and unfold (G).

Woven Paper

Draw lines the length of a sheet of coloured craft paper, ½ inch apart and leaving a border of one inch on each end (Fig. 10).

Place the paper on a breadboard or other indestructible surface. Use a safe craft razor (see page 13), and slit each line.

To weave, cut a series of ½-inch-wide strips (A), as long as the width of the paper "loom". Use a colour that contrasts or harmonises with the original paper, and weave in and out as shown. After *each* row, press gently against the finished section to avoid empty spaces. When the mat is finished paste down the loose ends of each strip.

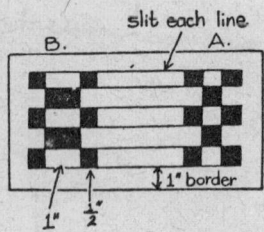

Fig. 10 Woven paper.

In B, alternate strips are one inch wide. Use one colour for the wide strips, another for the narrow.

Choose colour combinations to suit the room for which intended. Use for table mats, small chest or dresser mats. These can be made any size. Glue several together if paper is not large enough. Make a miniature size for a doll's house, using narrow strips.

Snowflake Design

Use a pencil compass or a small glass to cut a circle the size of the snowflake desired. Two inches across is a good size for a design (Fig. 11, A).

Fold the circle in half (B), then again in thirds (C), and fold the thirds into halves again (D).

If a stencil is desired, in order to transfer the snowflake

Crafts

design to another surface, cut as shown in E. *The main cuts are on the fold line.* This opens as shown in E, opened. The snowflake shown in dark background is within an unbroken circle.

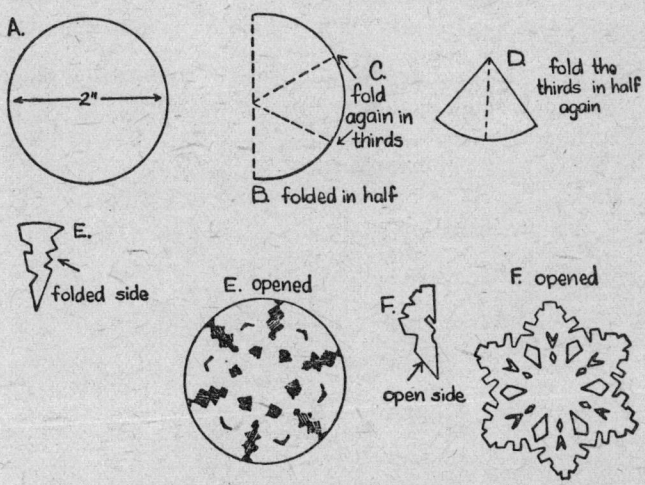

Fig. 11. Snowflake design.

If a snowflake outline is desired, to be pasted to other surfaces, cut the main design *along the open edge* as shown in F, with the folded edge cut just once or twice to add interest. This opens as shown in F, opened. Use snowflakes glued to coloured craft paper for Christmas ornaments; use for scrapbook designs, border designs, or paste in rows along the wall of a doll's house for wallpaper.

Wallpaper Ideas

1. Cut designs from wallpaper scraps, glue to the corners of plain cheap mats, varnish twice.

2. Cover a wastepaper basket. Varnish if desired.

3. Make a set of paper-plate pictures.

4. Use to decorate stationery.

5. Cut designs for birthday cards.

6. Cover a booklet box.

Stores where wallpaper is sold often have old samples they are willing to give away free.

Cut-Paper Designs

For creating a picture with designs cut from craft paper, choose, for a small picture, a 3-by-5 inch file card, or cut a circle of white cardboard using a large glass as a pattern. For a larger picture use a piece of craft paper for the background.

Fig. 12. Cut-paper design.

Draw the design first, the exact size of your planned picture. Make it simple, with easy cutting lines. Cut out each figure separately.

Trace the pattern pieces on coloured craft paper and cut out. Glue these to the background rectangle or circle (Fig. 12).

Torn-Paper Designs

The same as above, but *tear* the shapes, very carefully, instead of cutting them (Fig. 13).

Fig. 13. Torn paper design.

Shell Scene

Draw a scene and decorate with a variety of little shells. A shore scene is especially attractive. There could be blue water edged in sand, glued on, and sprinkled with groups of shells; perhaps also pavements, roads, a little house, made of shell.

Cutout Pictures

Use a piece of heavy craft paper for the background. Thumb through magazines for interesting items that are in proper scale with each other.

When a fair collection is ready, lay the pictures out and see how many can be used to create an attractive scene. Do not make it too cluttered, and draw in anything lacking, such as sun, sky, grass.

Collage

A collage is a solid picture made of small sections of many pictures, pasted together helter-skelter to tell a story.

To make a collage, decide on a subject. Use mail-order catalogues or magazines to find pictures to suit. Any subject will do: a family, the city, crops, careers, transportation; whatever appeals most. A collage of a family, for example, may show a house, partly covered by family members and their possessions, or family scenes such as watching TV or playing football together. Each scene is small, perhaps oddly shaped, half-covered by another, giving glimpses or snatches that suggest the theme.

Collages are much more attractive when all or some of the pictures are in colour.

Textured Painting

"Painting" with sawdust (from a timber merchant) creates an interesting texture. To prepare the sawdust, dye it (any except redwood or cedar) the colour desired by covering with poster paint. When the colour has soaked in, drain sawdust on newspaper and dry. Draw the outline of a picture on a cardboard back. Then spread paste on all the areas that are to be a certain colour: green, for example, such as grass and trees. Sprinkle the green sawdust on this. When dry, paste over the areas for another colour, and repeat until the textured area has been covered colour by colour. For better contrast cover only part of the picture with sawdust; perhaps just the figure, in front of a painted or crayon-coloured background. In this case, do the textured part last.

Variation: Experiment by adding dried ground coffee or sand, plus a little glue, to small quantities of poster paints.

Textured Crayon Pictures

Draw a picture with crayons, and when finished use as many materials as possible to give texture to it. A scene of a boy with a football, for example, could have a thin sponge goal behind him, the ball a flat circle of cotton of the thin layered type that comes in jewellery boxes. Clothes can be real fabrics glued on, but avoid porous materials such as linen, which shows the glue. Trees could be covered with tiny torn bits of green craft paper, glued on one over another like pebbles on a beach. The possibilities of ingenuity are almost unlimited.

For another use for this see "Shadow Box" in Chapter 4.

Crayon on Cloth

Use unworn sections of old sheeting. Colour a master design on paper, copy on the material and colour, pressing heavily with ordinary crayons. When finished place on newspaper, coloured side down, and iron with a warm wet cloth and hot iron. Use for designing doll items: curtains, bedspreads, dresser runners, etc., or for costumes.

Crayon-Scratch Designs

Use many different colours of crayons to create a design (rather than a picture) on a smooth paper. Colour over it solidly with black crayon. Open a paper clip and use this to scratch another design. This removes the black, permitting lines of colour to show through.

Crayon-and-Paint Designs

Draw a design of interesting lines by pressing heavily with a crayon, and then paint over the whole picture with thin poster paint. Or, draw anything you wish on black construction paper and paint over it with white poster paint, or draw on white paper and paint with black paint.

Marbleized Paper

Use the edge of scissors or a dull knife to scrape little chips of crayons of various colours onto a piece of paper. Cover with other paper and press with a rather hot iron.

Mosaics

A mosaic is a scene or design created by fitting together many small, varicoloured pieces.

TILE MOSAIC: For this you will need: sixty-four $\frac{3}{4}$ inch tiles, in several colours, found in hobby or tile shops; grout, a very inexpensive filler found in hardware, plumbing supply or hobby shops; a good glue; a $7\frac{1}{2}$-by-$7\frac{1}{2}$-inch (8-by-8-inch will do) piece of thin plywood.

Create a design first, in crayon colours, on graph paper. Any geometric pattern works well. When ready, begin at a corner of the plywood and work one row at a time, coating each tile underside with a layer of glue, and placing in position (Fig. 14, A). Tiles should be approximately $\frac{1}{8}$ inch apart. Allow twenty-four hours to dry, and then reglue any loose tiles if necessary, again allowing time to dry. Now

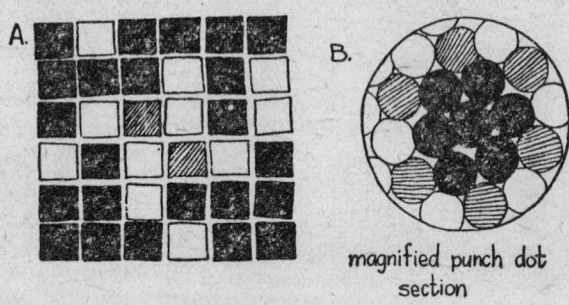

Fig. 14. Mosaics.

(A) Small tile mosaic (36 squares).
(B) Punch-dot mosaic.

seal the edges of the plywood with adhesive tape, preferably the flesh-coloured, shiny-finish type.

Mix powdered grout with water, adding a little at a time until a thick, whipped-cream consistency is reached. Pour carefully in the spaces between the tiles, pressing firmly until level with the tiles. Do not clean the tiles of the excess grout until it is fairly well set in the crevices.

Allow eight hours' drying time and then glue felt, or strips of felt, to the undersurface of the plywood.

This makes an excellent and attractive hot pad. A 4-by-4-inch size can be used as a drink coaster or under a vase.

PUNCH-DOT MOSAICS: Punch a number of dots from coloured craft paper with a paper punch. The larger the hole, the easier the work will be. Keep the colours separate. Design a pattern using different-coloured dots in lines, circles, diamonds, etc. Making a pattern on graph paper makes any type of design easier to execute.

Cut a 4-by-4-inch square of white cardboard. Cover lightly with glue, a section at a time. With a pin lightly prick and pick up a dot of the proper colour. Place in one corner of cardboard and work away from it, or in the centre as shown in Fig. 14, B, until the square is complete.

Apply design to both sides for a mobile decoration. Or use as a wall ornament. Or varnish twice (let dry before second coat), and use as a coaster. Four coasters, all different in design, make an attractive gift.

BUTTON MOSAICS: Cut a square of cardboard, 4-by-4-inches or 8-by-8 inches as desired. Lay out old buttons in a design. If there are enough to make a solid pattern, cover the cardboard with glue and, following the laid-out design, place buttons in position. If there is a space between the buttons, first cover the cardboard with craft paper and then glue on the buttons.

DECORATIONS AND ACCESSORIES

To Wear

EARRINGS: Make earrings of stiff cardboard painted on both sides with nail enamel or other paint. They can be any unusual shape desired, and may be decorated with sequins, beads or glitter, glued on. Round earrings for pirates, gypsies, and so on can be made of cardboard covered with foil.

When finished, glue or punch holes near the top of the earrings. Through holes, attach a small loop of string that just fits the ear. Slip over the entire ear (Fig. 15, A).

BRACELET: Cut a 2-by-6-inch band of thin cardboard. Decorate with a design done in several shades of nail enamel or enamel paint. Or cover with oddly shaped bits of brightly coloured gummed crêpe paper, to create a mosaic design. This can be varnished or covered with colourless nail enamel if desired (Fig. 15, B).

Fasten by stringing ribbon through two holes on each end, tying inside the wrist.

BEADS:

1. Make beads of macaroni. This can be coloured if dip-

ped quickly in and out of water with food colouring. When thoroughly dry string with cotton carpet thread, twine or shoelace. Stiffen the end of the string with glue or tightly wind with Sellotape (Fig. 15, C).

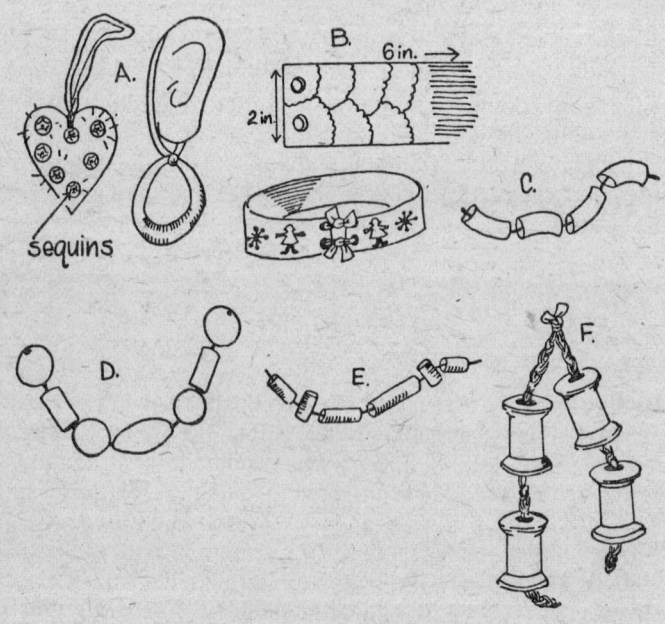

Fig. 15. Jewellery.

(A) Earrings, with strings to be slipped over ear.
(B) Bracelets.
(C) Macaroni beads.
(D) Dough beads.
(E) Drinking-straw beads.
(F) Cotton reel beads.

2. Use modelling or play dough. (To make play dough, mix one cup flour, one cup salt and slightly under one cup of water as needed.) Colour the dough several colours. Mould beads in a number of sizes and shapes to create interest (Fig. 15, D). For variety make a number of marbleized beads by kneading just long enough to hold

Crafts

together well a small ball of each colour. Make a stringing hole in each bead while wet, using a needle or toothpick. Allow to dry several days before stringing.

3. Cut drinking straws of several colours into various lengths (Fig. 15, E).

4. Cotton reels. Paint with non-lead paint. To string, braid three 40-inch strands of cotton togeher; tie at one end with a large knot; stiffen the other end with Sellotape or glue (Fig. 15, F).

Give the cotton reel beads to a small child for a gift. If painted different colours you can help him learn the colours by playing a game, lining them up by colour. Or teach numbers by having him count the number of beads of each colour. He will enjoy stringing them himself.

For the Home

PETAL FLOWERS: Stick two sheets of gummed crêpe paper back to back, or use one thickness of craft paper. Cut circles of different sizes, using drinking glass bottoms for patterns. Scallop the edges (Fig. 16, A) or fringe (B) by cutting towards the centre with scissors. Glue a small circle of another colour in the centre. Curl the petals as shown (C), over a knitting needle or matchstick. Glue a green crêpe or craft paper leaf to the back.

Use on a mobile, or on cards, or for textured pictures. Or tape several in a group to a mirror for a party decoration.

CARNATION: This is very easily made and looks real when finished.

Fold one doubled face tissue in half lengthwise, and accordion-pleat, about ½ inch for each pleat (Fig. 17, A). When pleated cut off the folded edge (B). Tie the centre tightly (C) with picture wire, thread, or narrow ribbon.

There will be four layers of tissue on each side. Very carefully pull these apart, and the carnation is made (D).

For a stem, attach a garden "Twistem" wire to the tie at the centre, or use florists' wire, green ribbon or green pipe cleaners curled by winding around a pencil.

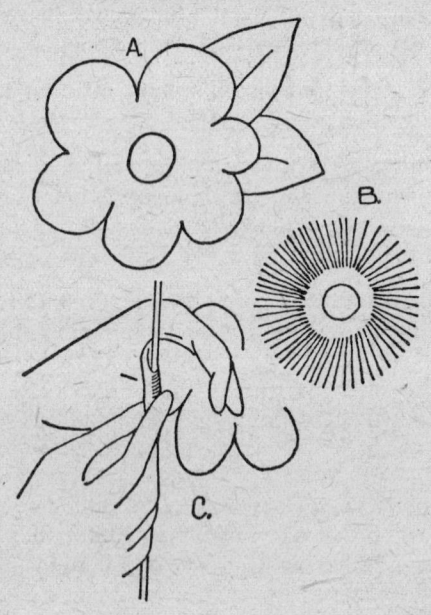

Fig. 16. (A) Petal flower, made of a scalloped circle of craft or crepe paper.
(B) Fringed flower.
(C) How to curl flower edges over a small stick.

For coloured carnations use coloured face tissue. Pink or white tissues may be very lightly streaked on the outer edges with nail polish to add variety and colour. If desired the edges may be pinked, in step B, but this makes the pulling-apart somewhat more difficult.

Variation: Toilet tissue works equally well and also comes in colour. Three double sheets, separated, laid one on top of the other and then accordion-pleated and tied, form a flower about the size of a face-tissue flower. For a miniature carnation lay two double sheets together, cut to any size desired, and accordion-pleat in $\frac{1}{4}$ inch folds. Toilet tissues cut in half lengthwise make a pretty miniature.

Crafts

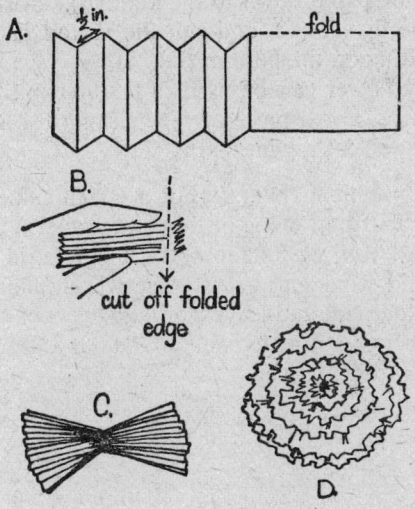

Fig. 17. Carnation.

CREPE-PAPER FLOWERS: For a flower ½ inch in diameter, cut a piece of crêpe paper ½ by 2 inches. Run a tacking stitch as shown (Fig. 18, A), then pull the tacking thread

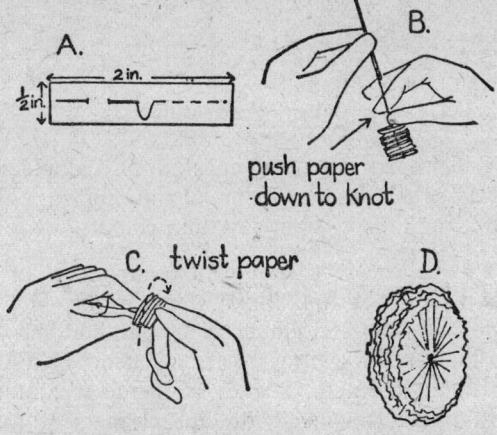

Fig. 18. Crepe-paper flower.

while pushing paper down to the knot (B). Twist the paper to form the flower (C), and run the thread back through again, knotting on the bottom (D).

This tiny flower can be used in textured pictures or on greeting cards. Use a piece of pipe cleaner for a stem. For a larger flower cut a wider strip.

CATHERINE WHEEL FLOWERS: For a ¼ inch catherine wheel flower, cut a strip of crêpe or thin craft paper 6 by ¼ inches (Fig. 19, A). Roll or fold to make a long strip as thin as possible, and wind into a catherine wheel, gluing the end (B). Draw the stem and leaves, or cut slivers of green crêpe or craft paper and paste to background (C). Use for textured pictures or cards.

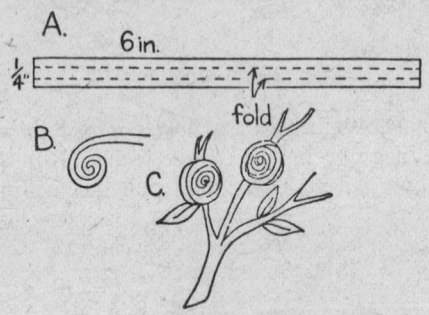

Fig. 19. Catherine wheel flowers.

TULIPS: Cut the individual egg cups out of a moulded egg carton. Scallop the sides that are not already cut (Fig. 20, A). Poster-paint the little cups in gay tulip colours.

Fill a cottage cheese carton with sand, gravel or soil, and cover with silver foil. Make stems by bending pipe cleaners down ½ inch and gluing to the cup bottoms. Push them into the sand in a pleasing arrangement (B). Be sure the stems differ in length. Leaves are made separately of green craft paper stiffened with pipe cleaners or garden "Twistem" glued to the backs.

Crafts 35

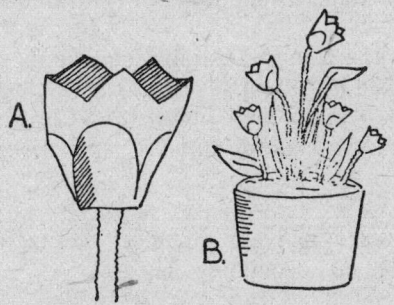

Fig. 20. Tulips.

THE FLOWER TREE: Make seven or more white carnations (see page 31). With the lightest of strokes streak the edges with red or pink nail polish.

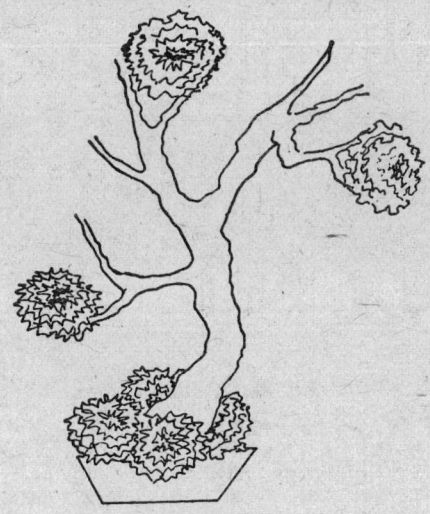

Fig. 21. Flower tree.

Spray a deadwood branch white, and stand upright in clay or polystyrene. Cluster four flowers around the base; wire the rest to the branches (Fig. 21). Place on a table or dresser top. Replace the flowers when no longer fresh-looking.

Variations: Use coloured tissues to suit the room colours, or white streaked in gold or silver. Use the same deadwood branch for seasonal decorations such as Christmas ornaments, Easter eggs, Hallowe'en craft-paper designs.

Pictures and Frames

PICTURE FRAMES: Here are a number of suggestions for framing pictures and decorating the edges.

1. Fold bright-coloured craft paper into three parts. Glue a picture into each section (Fig. 22, A).

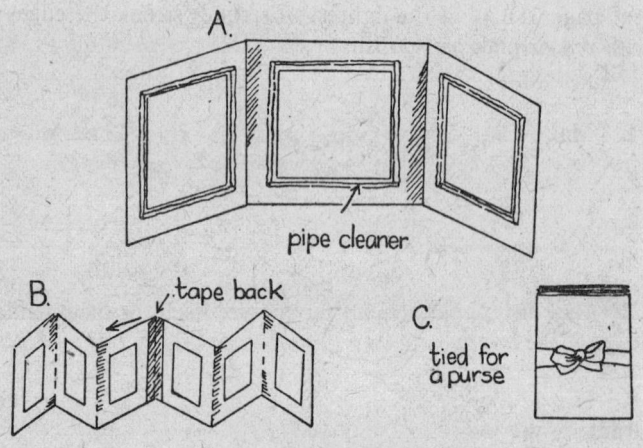

Fig. 22. Picture frames.

(A) Sectional.
(B) For a series of pictures.
(C) Frame folded to carry in purse.

2. Cut two strips of craft paper 11 inches long and 2 inches wider than the height of the pictures you wish to frame. Glue or sellotape the two strips together as shown (B). Beginning at the taped fold (see arrow), measure off a section 2 inches wider than the pictures to be framed.

Crafts

Accordion-fold from the taped middle, working each direction, as shown. Cut off any excess paper at the ends. Glue a picture into each section. Tie with a ribbon to carry in purse (C).

3. Glue a picture to heavy cardboard, about an inch larger than the picture all around. Cut a piece of craft paper, burlap felt, or other interesting material the size of the cardboard. Cut an oval, rectangular or circular hole in the material and glue to the cardboard to frame the picture.

4. Frame a picture with a doily, cutting a suitable hole in the centre. Glue to coloured craft paper if desired. Tie a ribbon to the top for hanging.

To decorate the frames of these pictures, use one of the following suggestions:

1. Make holes every $\frac{1}{4}$ or $\frac{1}{2}$ inch all around and lace a ribbon in and out, tying at the top with a bow (Fig. 23, A).

2. Glue a continuous edging of lace or velvet ribbon around either the picture or the frame.

3. Glue tiny shells around the picture itself, or the outside edge of the frame.

4. Use a pipe cleaner in a colour that contrasts with the frame — white on red, for example.

5. Sponge-paint the border.

6. Frame with a border print made of white paper for a coloured frame or coloured paper for a white frame.

To make frame stand, cut a strip of heavy cardboard, $\frac{1}{2}$ inch wide and one inch longer than half the height of the picture. Bend strip as shown (Fig. 23, B), glue to frame, and extend behind picture.

STAND-UP PICTURES: Cut out any magazine pictures that might be used in a game: people, furniture, cars, houses, etc. Paste these on cardboard and lay under a heavy object to dry. Then cut the cardboard to the shape of the picture and a second cardboard exactly like it. Connect these at the top with sellotape, open at the bottom, and the picture will stand alone (Fig. 23 C).

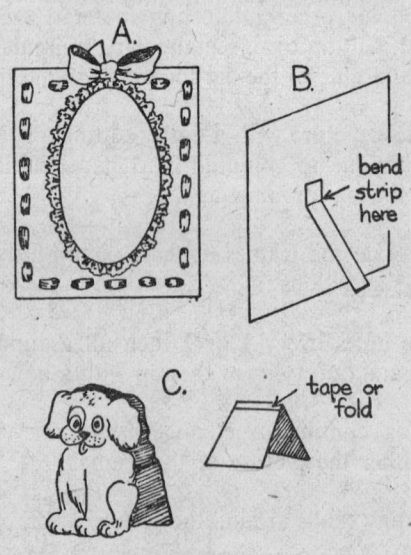

Fig. 23. (A) Ways of decorating a picture frame.
(B) Cardboard strip glued to the back of a picture to permit standing.
(C) Stand-up pictures for use in a game.

Variations: The same idea can be used with crayon pictures. Fold a piece of heavy paper, and then draw the picture to the top of the fold. Cut the paper to the outline of the picture, being careful *not* to cut the folded top edge. The picture will then stand alone (Fig. 23, C).

Mobiles

A mobile is a freely hanging design that moves with any breeze.

Crafts 39

The very simplest type is a single light-weight craft item, such as a bird or flower, suspended from the ceiling with a thread. Other mobiles:

WIRE CLOTHES HANGER: Hang four or five ribbons or threads of varying lengths from the wire, each holding an object (Fig. 24, A).

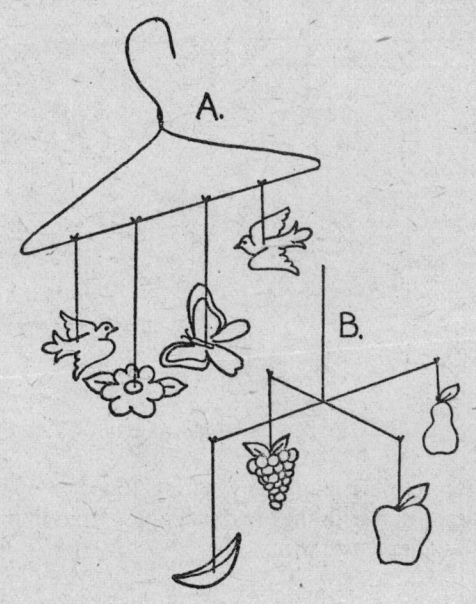

Fig. 24. Mobiles.

(A) Clothes-hanger mobile.
(B) Crossed-wire mobile.

CROSSED WIRE: Twist one wire at right angles to another and suspend an object from each corner, all at different balanced lengths (B).

TRIANGLE MOBILE:* Cut five wires in the following lengths (Fig. 25, A): (1) the spiral, 18 inches; (2) 36 inches; (3) 18

---

* From *Fun With Crafts*, p. 27; used with permission of the Dennison Manufacturing Co., Framingham, Mass.

40   555 Ways To Amuse Your Child

inches; (4) 36 inches; (5) 27 inches. These can be wound with strips of crêpe paper if desired. Form the top spiral; bend wires into thirds (B), hook over one another as illus-

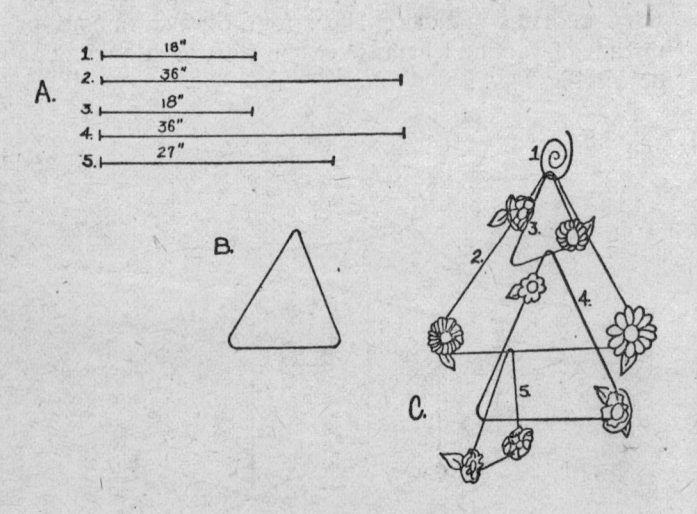

A.
1. |——— 18" ———|
2. |——————— 36" ———————|
3. |——— 18" ———|
4. |——————— 36" ———————|
5. |————— 27" —————|

B.

C.

Fig. 25.   Triangle mobile.

trated (C), close triangles by wiring together with picture wire or covering with more crêpe paper. Hold in the proper positions with picture wire.

To decorate any of the above mobiles, use birds below, paper flowers and papier-mâché fruit, craft paper decorated on both sides or any other light-weight, pretty objects. They can be made seasonal by using paper eggs at Easter, ornaments at Christmas.

Hang the mobiles by suspending from a screw in the ceiling or a beam, or from a bracket extended from the wall.

Birds

1. To make a decorative bird, draw pattern on graph paper, using Figure 26 as a model. Cut out wings (A) and body (B) of felt, thin layers of polystyrene, foil or craft

Crafts

paper. (Foil can be curved into the most realistic shape but will hold better if stapled where glue is suggested.)

Staple or glue the darkened area of the pipe cleaner C-3, *under* the darkened area A-2. Staple or glue B-1 *over* A-2. If glued, set aside to dry. When ready, glue B-4 to B-5. Use very small beads or contrasting bits of foil or other paper

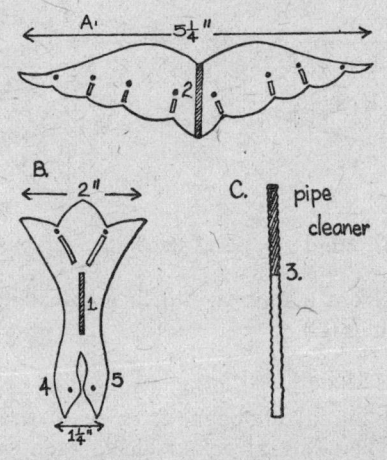

Fig. 26. Bird for a tree ornament, candle or mobile.

for eyes. Run lines of glue along the small outlined rectangles on the wings (A) and tail (B) and sprinkle with sparkle. Shake off excess. If desired, glue sequins where dots are shown.

Leave the long end on the pipe cleaner to attach the bird to a mobile (see above) candle or Christmas tree.

2. On graph paper draw the body, wings, and tail of the bird shown in Fig. 27. Then transfer design to craft paper. Colour in the eye. Moisten the edges of the tail, wings and beak with glue and sprinkle with glitter. Cut a slot just behind the head (Fig. 27, A), to insert wings, and staple or glue firmly. Cut tail slot (A), insert tail and glue to position.

Hang several of these from a mobile (see above), flower tree, or the Christmas tree, or use as spring party invitations.

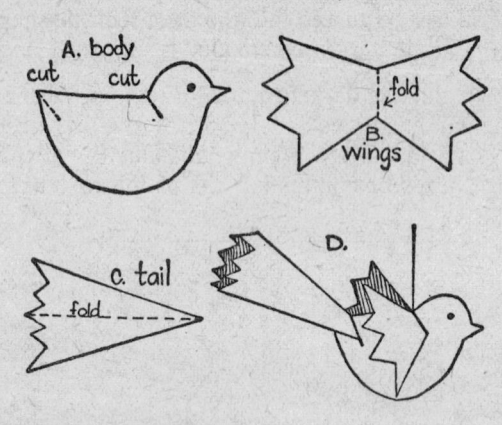

Fig. 27. Bird for party decoration or mobile.

To suspend from a mobile, attach a thread to the body behind the wings (D).

Stained-Glass Medallions

Save up coloured cellophane from sweet wrappings and elsewhere. When several colours have been saved, use a compass or a plate to draw a 6-inch circle on black craft paper. Cut out circle and use a sharp craft razor to cut

Fig. 28. Stained-glass medallion. Each section is a different colour of cellophane or tissue paper.

designs in the circle. The black areas shown in Fig. 28 are the uncut black background remaining. Use the pieces cut away as patterns to cut the different colours of cellophane,

Crafts

but cut each cellophane piece ⅛ *inch larger than the pattern* all the way around. Cover the black background with glue and glue the cellophane over the openings.

Hang in a window where it will catch the light, or give as a gift. The medallion can be cut in the shape of a cross, a diamond, a triangle etc. Coloured tissue paper may be used instead of cellophane.

Wall Bowl of Fruit

Buy a small individual wooden salad bowl. Make miniature fruits of papier-mâché or clay. While still wet, insert stems made of bits of twig, wire covered with gummed green crêpe paper or florist's wire saved from bouquets. Paint fruit with poster paints when dry.

Fig. 29. Wall bowl of fruit.

Glue these firmly to the bottom of the bowl in a pleasing arrangement (Fig. 29). Three or four leaves can be tucked behind fruit if desired. Make these of gummed crêpe paper glued back to back, or craft paper.

If preferred, long wire stems can be attached to the fruit while still soft, and these can be caught together and the entire bunch of fruit glued in as a unit.

Attach a picture hanger to the back of the bowl and hang in the kitchen or breakfast room.

Free-Form Wax Designs

Use old candles or paraffin. If there is not enough colour, add wax crayons. (To be sure crayons are wax, scrape with the nail. Wax will curl off in chips.) Heat the candles and crayons until melted, then pour a thin layer of wax into an individual pie or tart tin made of foil. (These are more easily managed by young children. Older children can manage full-size tins.) Let cool about one minute then dip the tins of wax in a tub or plastic pool. (It is preferable to work outdoors with this.) Hold hands and elbows well *out*, not *up*, or wax will spurt up the arm.

When the tin is pushed into water rapidly, the wax billows suddenly into "sails". When done slowly it forms into rounded moons. These are lovely forms for use alone in decorating, or with flowers or natural arrangements.

Decorated Bottles

SMALL: Soak off the label from a pretty bottle such as pills or household supplies sometimes come in. Use nail polish to paint the name of a spice, cake decorating item, sugar substitute etc., on one side (Fig. 30).

Fig. 30. Small decorated bottles.

Paint a pretty all-over design or a border of spidery lines. Or paint a wide bright line around top or bottom.

LARGE: Have ready a number of dried egg shells broken into many small pieces. Choose a nicely shaped bottle. Paint with enamel of any colour desired — perhaps a colour that would look well in the living room as a vase or decoration or in the bathroom with bath salts. While still wet, sprinkle all over with eggshells, or carefully press them on in a design (Fig. 31).

Crafts

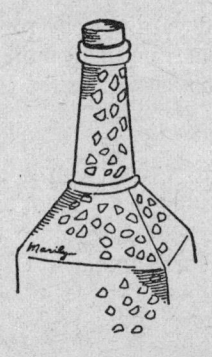

Fig. 31. Large decorated bottle.

Variation: Cover bottle with flat paint (indoor gloss paint), and while wet carefully add sequins, beads, small pretty buttons, or sparkle. Or use cotton, bits of felt or foil, or any other decorating material. Have the materials ready ahead of time, and before beginning draw a simple design on paper to follow in general as you work. A pin is helpful in placing the small decorations.

If the bottle has no stopper find a cork to suit. Paint to match the bottle and then decorate it, or cover with glue and decorate. Use a funnel to fill with bath salts.

Pencil Holders

A small can covered with wool makes a pencil holder for desk or telephone. Cover the top inch of outside of can

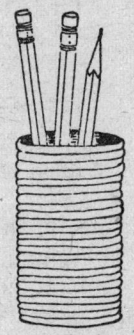

Fig. 32. Pencil holder.

with glue and wind yarn row by row, being sure each is close to the previous row. Add more glue and yarn until finished, changing colours if desired (Fig. 32).

Vase

Find a pretty jar. Cover with a design, using several colours of thick poster paint chosen to harmonise with the room for which the vase is intended. When dry coat with varnish, if desired, for permanence.

Enamel paint or several shades of old nail polish may be substituted instead.

Decorated Containers

Use small-size round boxes or cartons. First, measure the carton up to the lid (shown by arrows, Fig. 33, A). Cut a piece of bright craft paper or wrapping paper as wide as the arrows indicate, and as long as the circumference of the

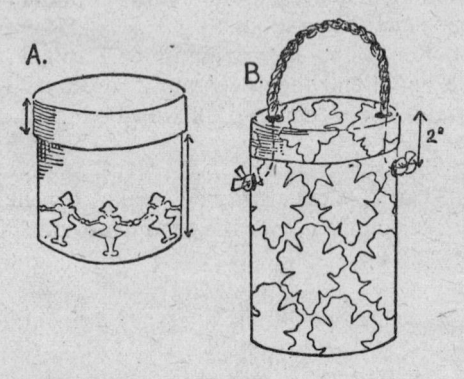

Fig. 33. (A) Decorated container.
(B) Knitting bag.

box. Cut a matching strip to fit the side of the lid (small arrows), and a circle to fit the top. To do this turn the lid upside down and draw around, then cut about 1/16 inch inside this line. Carefully paste these pieces on the box, smoothing out air holes.

If plain paper is used, decorate with a border print or paint a design if desired.

For a string holder, cut a small round hole in the top. This box can be used also as a container for biscuits, sweets, wool or sewing items.

Variation: Make a knitting bag by using a large box and fastening a handle as shown in Fig. 33, B.

GIFTS TO GIVE

In addition to the suggestions below, many of the items described elsewhere in this book make excellent gifts. See in particular "Toys of Paper and Paste", later in this chapter.

Surprise Ball

A surprise ball is one package made of strips of crêpe paper and holding many small surprises. These can be individually wrapped if desired.

To make, leave crêpe paper folded in the package and cut off 2-inch strips. Start with four strips, in differing colours if possible, adding as many as needed. Lay out about ten or twelve small items, to suit the person for which it is intended: chewing gum, wrapped sweets, miniature cars and men, dolls or furniture, pencils — anything small. Start with the longest item. Wind this in a strip of crêpe paper until covered. Add the bulkiest items next, by laying one at a time beside the wrapped items, wrapping each in turn with the crêpe windings. Sellotape wherever necessary to hold strips in place.

When finished it will look like a crêpe paper "ball" (Fig. 34, A). When the recipient opens it, he will uncover only one gift at a time.

If desired, the finished surprise ball may be decorated.

Wrapped in a large handkerchief and attached to a stick (B), the ball could be used as a prize at a "tramps" party or going-away gift.

48   *555 Ways To Amuse Your Child*

Fig. 34. Surprise balls.

The chequered surprise ball (C) is filled with trinkets and wrapped in a little tablecloth made of a square yard or metre of chequered material, and tiny matching napkins are used as decoration. It could be given to a girl convalescent with the trinkets wrapped in different colours of crêpe paper and instructions to unwind only one colour each day.

The clown (D) could be a boy's birthday gift. The head is cut from an old birthday card. Shoes are made of cardboard, coloured black except for "holes", and bent at the instep.

For other Surprise Balls, create a decoration using pictures from old cards or magazine pictures stiffened with cardboard.

Crafts

Decorated Stationery

Buy plain white notepaper. Cut small designs from scraps of cloth and glue to a corner of each piece (Fig. 35).

Fig. 35. Decorated stationery.

To make a fine gift for someone with an autumn birthday, cut small designs from old Christmas cards and glue to stationery.

Penwipers

Use scraps of flannel or woollen material, and pinking shears if available. Make a paper pattern. This can measure approximately 5 inches both ways, but can be shaped like a circle, a butterfly, a car, etc. (Fig. 36). Using the paper pattern, cut two designs if the material is heavy, three or four designs if light. Stitch these together firmly in the

Fig. 36. Penwipers.

middle, leaving the edges free to slip a pen between to clean the nib.

Basket Bag

Buy a plain small wicker or straw bag. Decorate it with small shells, beads, or old artificial flowers or fruits that can be separated and used individually. Choose colours to suit the clothes to be worn with it. Plan a design first on paper, and use household glue to place decorations.

Sewing Box

Get a wooden cigar box, pull out the inside lining and soak off the label with a warm damp cloth — not too long, or the wood will warp.

Choose for a lining a sturdy material that will not show dirt (oilcloth, plastic, canvas, denim). From this cut a strap 2 by 4 inches to strengthen the lid. Fold the strap lengthwise and stitch the edges under. Glue to lid and side as shown (Fig. 37).

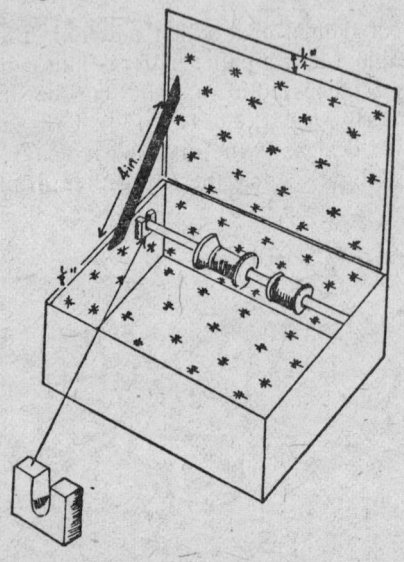

Fig. 37. Sewing box.

Measure the sides of the box accurately and cut pieces of lining material the exact sizes of front, bottom and back. Glue into the box and bind the corners with gummed plastic tape to match the material. Be careful not to go over the rim or the box will not close tightly. The lid lining should end $\frac{1}{4}$ inch from the front edge and $\frac{1}{8}$ from each side for the lid to close tightly. If you have no plastic tape cut the linings $\frac{1}{4}$ inch larger all around, glue hems under or stitch on the machine, and then glue to the box.

Paint the outside of the box with enamel, using one of the colours of the lining. Decorate the lid with pipe-cleaner letters spelling the recipient's name, or bits of felt cut in a design, or shells, or anything else desired. If felt is used, designs could be sewing symbols: scissors, buttons, cotton reels, etc.

For a cotton reel rod, measure the exact inside width of the box. Use a piece of dowelling this length and $\frac{1}{4}$ inch diameter. Hold in position with two rubbers or tiny blocks of wood glued one inch from the top. One rubber must have an opening cut from the rod hole of the rubber to the top, to insert the rod (see Fig. 37).

Fit this box with small boxes for pins and buttons, embroidery thread and the like.

Jewelled Box

Use a little plastic box, the colourless, transparent type such as many items come in. Glue sequins, fake jewels (may be taken from old earrings), pipe cleaners, or shells to the lid for decoration (Fig. 38). Plan the pattern first on paper.

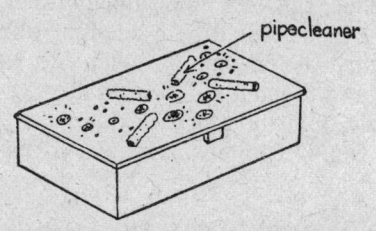

Fig. 38. Girl's or woman's jewelled box.

If soaking the box removes the advertising paper but not the glue, cover the same area with an attractively shaped piece of bright-coloured felt. This can be decorated as above. If it is to be used as a dressing table ornament choose a colour that suits the room, and glue tiny strips of felt on both ends of the bottom to prevent scratching the furniture.

Accessories Box

Small transparent plastic cigar or other boxes make attractive accessories boxes for male relatives or family members. Soak off the paper nameplate. Cut an oval or other design of felt and glue to the top. Glue a small toy pipe (or any

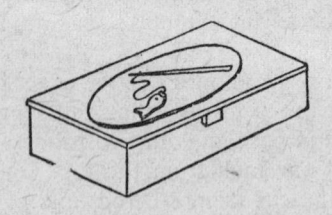

Fig. 39. Boy's or man's accessories box.

other masculine ware) to the felt. Or glue other colours of felt, cut in the motif of a favourite sport (Fig. 39). Line with scrap flannel, felt, velvet, or a layer of cotton. Glue two strips of felt to the bottom to protect furniture.

Plastic Purse Envelope

This is for carrying all the miscellaneous lists, receipts and extra cards that will not fit into a card holder or wallet, or for purse face tissues. Choose a plain plastic bag approximately 5 by 10 inches. Tape a one-foot ribbon along one side of the top extending out on either side. Use nail enamel or enamel paint to paint a design on the bag. To hold contents securely, fold the top back down and tie the ribbon around the bag. Decorate with sequins if desired.

Doorstop

Cover a brick with oilcloth. Use a colour that suits the

room, and blanket-stitch the edges with a contrasting colour. Cut designs from patterned material and glue on.

Book Ends

Fig. 40. Felt-covered brick book end.

For a pair of heavy book ends, cover two bricks with felt, using a blanket stitch in a contrasting colour. Make designs with other colours of felt, and glue on (Fig. 40).

Litter Bag

Use a *heavy* plain plastic bag approximately 8 by 12 inches. Tape a loop of ribbon about 6 inches long to one corner of the top. Tape all edges, for strength. Coloured sellotape or plastic tape is fine for this. Paint a design using household enamel or nail enamel, or tape a design.

Give as a gift to hang in the car, for holding rubbish.

HOUSES AND DOLLS

Paper House

Cut an 8 or 8½ inch square of paper. Fold in half along line 1 (Fig. 41, A), in half again along line 2. Open; refold very lightly along line 3 and then 4. Cut dotted lines as shown.

54   555 Ways To Amuse Your Child

Colour the four centre "roof" sections, drawing in the direction shown. Cut out the windows (shown as squares) with small nail scissors or craft razor, or just colour them. Cut the door along the dotted lines only.

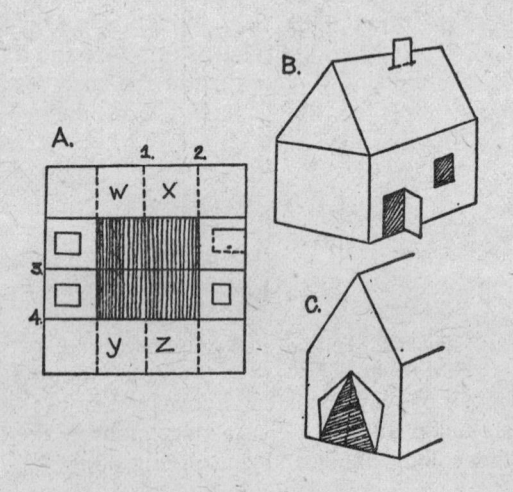

Fig. 41.   (A and B)   Paper house.
          (C)   Tent.

Now fold square *x* completely over square *w* and paste. Fold square *y* over *z* and paste, and the house is finished (B). To make a chimney, cut a very small slit across the roof top and insert a small square of red paper.

To make a miniature house for a tiny scene use a 4-inch square of paper.

Tent

To make a tent, follow directions given in Fig. 41 for a house, but omit colouring the roof. Leave out windows, door and chimney. When complete, cut a vertical slit through the pasted square *wx*; fold back for an opening (Fig. 41, C).

For another tent, see "Toys of Paper and Paste" page 78.

Crafts 55

Shoe-Box House

When small houses are needed for doll's houses or to create miniature towns, farms etc., for play with miniature men, use shoe boxes.

To make, turn upside down and cut the bottom of the box around the three dotted lines as shown in Fig. 42, A, for a hinged roof to permit placing of furniture and dolls or men. Glue the top rim of the box, now the base, to the lid (B), or tape it on the inside with plastic or adhesive tape. Colour the sides of the lid to resemble bricks or natural stone.

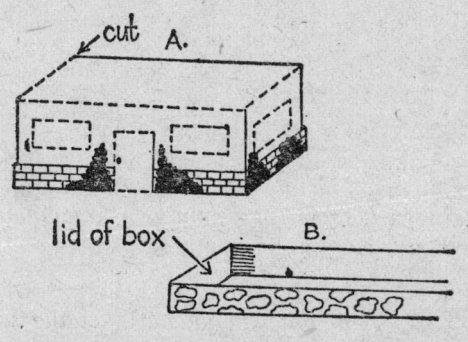

Fig. 42. Shoe-box house.

Cut windows and doors on dotted lines. Paint the box with poster paints or house paint. Paint the roof a contrasting colour if possible. Glue tiny sprigs of lichen or sphagnum moss from a hobby shop or the woods, to resemble plants coming up from the brick or stone base, or cut small bushes from green paper and glue on. Paint on window frames, walls and floor.

Shoe-Box Village

This Village can be easily packed away in a carton, with church, school, and peaked-roof types on top.

Follow general suggestions given for a shoe-box house, above, but vary for these buildings:

MODERN CHURCH: Turn the box with an end for the front. In this end cut an arched door; cut arched windows on the sides; colour or paste small "stained glass" windows in their

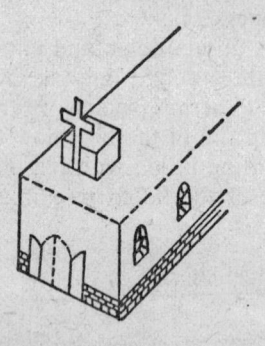

Fig. 43. Shoe-box church.

place. Cut a slit in the roof just large enough to hold a little cardboard cross, or firmly glue a small box to the roof, and paste a cross on it (Fig. 43).

INN: Glue or tape a lollipop stick to the inside of the hinged roof, so that it will jut out over the street as in

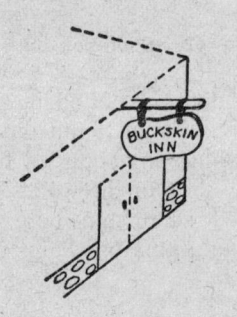

Fig. 44. Shoe-box inn.

Fig. 44. Paint if desired. From this tie two strings, or thin leather thongs, and a small board or cardboard. This can be cut into any special shape, such as an animal head, and

Crafts 57

should have a name (such as "The Stag", or "Buckskin Inn") as shown.

GROCERY SHOP: Print a name across the front, up near the roof. Cut a wide double door, paint in a long window with

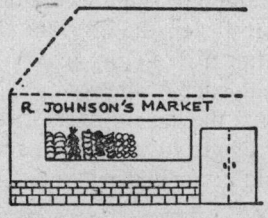

Fig. 45. Grocery shop.

fruits, vegetables, etc. (Fig. 45). If preferred, this could be a general store. Inside, small boxes can be placed on their sides or glued into position to form counters.

RANCH-STYLE HOUSE: Follow procedure in Fig. 46, A. Cut

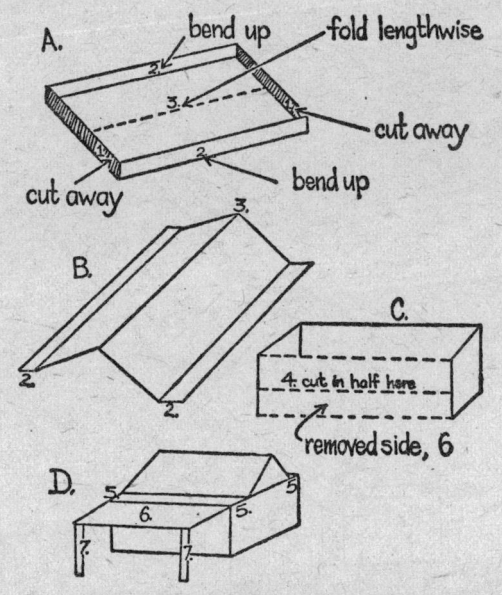

Fig. 46. Shoe-box ranch house.

both ends (1) from a shoe-box lid. Bend sides (2) up. Score with a knife and bend lengthwise along the centre line (3). When finished, the lid (house roof) will resemble Fig. 46, B.

Now cut one side (6) from the box (see Fig. 46, C) and cut the removed side in half lengthwise along line 4.

Use plastic tape to fasten the lid sides (2) flat to the top of the box (5), creating a roof (Fig. 46, D). Tape half of the cut-off side (6) to one edge of the roof as shown in D. This creates a porch. Tape the cut-off ends of the lid (1), shortened to the proper length, to the porch roof as pillars (7).

To store away, fold porch under.

BARN: This requires twin shoe-boxes in order to obtain two lids.

With each lid, cut off the ends (1) as in Fig. 47, A. Bend one side up (2). The lids are taped firmly together on the

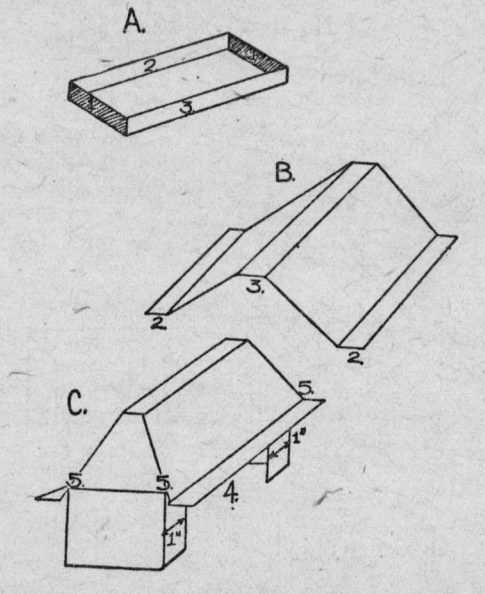

Fig. 47. Shoe-box barn.

Crafts

remaining side (3), creating a high roof as shown (Fig. 47, B).

Cut one side from the box bottom (Fig. 47, C), leaving one inch around the upper and side borders to avoid weakening the box (4).

Securely plastic-tape the roof to the box at four points (5).

Shoe-Box House Furnishings

BEDS: Make of papier mâché. For beds, a small matchbox slider is the right size for miniature dolls.

To make legs, cut the ends from four matches, push through the corners of the box, extend to ¼ inch below the bottom, cut off even with the top of the box, and glue (Fig. 48, A).

For a headboard, cut a piece of cardboard the exact width of the box and twice as high and glue into position. Paint or paper entire box, or cover headboard with a scrap of pretty fabric glued on. (See Doll's House, later in this section.)

MATTRESS: Cut a piece of old sheet that is *twice as wide* as the box — plus ½ inch, and just as long as the box — plus ½ inch. Fold lengthwise. Stitch inside out along end and side, leaving one end open. Turn right side out, stuff with a bit of cotton, turn the remaining edge inside and stitch across the end.

PILLOW: Follow mattress pattern except for size.

SHEETS: Two pieces of old sheeting cut the size of the bed, plus ½ inch all the way around for hems and tuck-in.

BLANKETS: Small scraps of wool or felt. These can be buttonhole-stitched around the edge if desired. (See "Sewing Stitches", page 104.)

BEDSPREAD: A piece of pretty material cut the size of the sheets and hemmed. If it is to be tucked under the pillows, add ½ inch to the length.

SETTEE: Make of papier mâché or clay, and paint (Fig. 48,

B). Rub excess paint off if clay is used. A padded seat and back can be made by covering with a thin layer of cotton wool and gluing material over this.

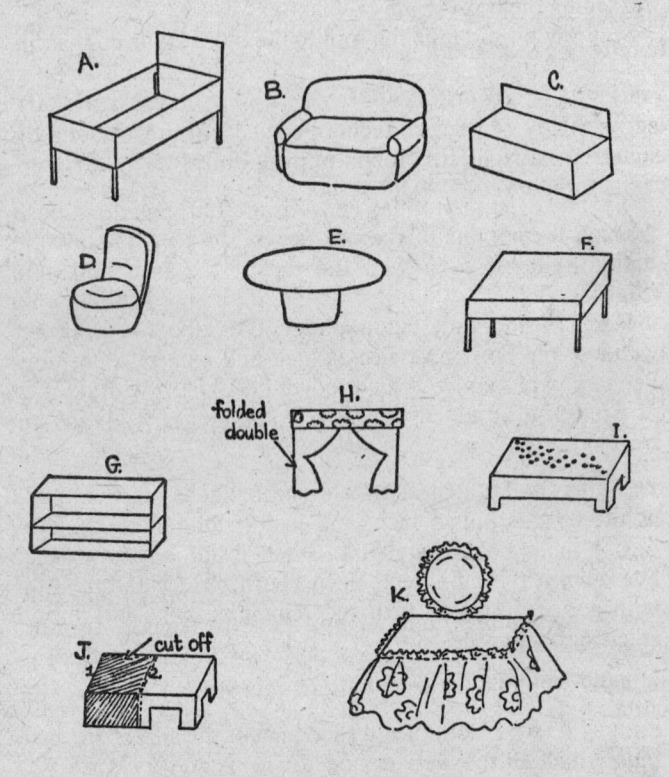

Fig. 48. Furnishings for a shoe-box house.

(A) Bed.
(B) Settee.
(C) Bench.
(D) Chair.
(E and F) Tables
(G) Bookcase.
(H) Curtains.
(I) Coffee table.
(J) Side table.
(K) Dressing table.

Crafts

BENCH: Make of clay or papier mâché, or cut a small matchbox slider in half lengthwise (C). Paste on a cardboard back and paint or cover with a scrap of cloth or plastic.

CHAIRS: Make of a round piece of clay or papier mâché, big enough to hold a miniature man, with a thumb-indentation for the seat and a barrel-shaped back (Fig. 48, D).

TABLES: For a round dining table with one centre (pedestal) leg, use clay or papier mâché (Fig. 48, E). Make it tall enough for a seated toy figure. Make four armless barrel chairs as above.

For a rectangular table, use clay or papier mâché, or a small matchbox slider turned upside down with matchstick legs glued to the inside of the box (Fig. 48, F). Paint any of these.

BOOKCASES: Several small matchbox sliders may be cut as for benches, above, but glued or taped one on top of the other (Fig. 48, G). For books cut cardboard rectangles small enough to fit on the shelves, glue three or four of these together to give thickness for each "book", and paint different colours.

CURTAINS: Cut bits of fabric double (Fig. 48, H), so that when folded and glued together at the top, the curtains will look pretty both inside and out. Glue to window frames. A valance may be made if desired by gluing a narrow strip of material above the window, covering the tops of the curtains also.

DISHES: Mould tiny dishes of clay, or make foil dishes by shaping foil around the end of your finger and flattening the bottom.

COFFEE TABLE: Cut out the sides of a small matchbox slider (Fig. 48, I). Paint. When dry decorate with punch-dot mosaics for a "tile" top.

SIDE TABLES: Use a matchbox slider cut in half (Fig. 48, J), with the cut-off side (1) glued or taped at the double-dotted line (2). Decorate to match the coffee table if desired.

DRESSING TABLE: Use a small box, or cut down a small matchbox as for an end table, above. Cut a scrap of cloth as wide as the height of the dressing table and 8 inches long. Sew with loose running stitches and gather into a ruffle, then glue to the top rim of the box for a flounce (Fig. 48, K).

For a mirror, see "Doll's House Decorations", later in this section.

CHESTS: Follow instructions for dresser chests (see under Doll's House Furniture), using small matchboxes.

KITCHEN APPLIANCES: Make of clay or papier mâché and paint.

BATHROOM APPLIANCES: Make of clay or papier mâché and paint.

See also "Doll's House Decorations" for the following: centrepieces, mirrors, lamps, indoor potted plants, pictures, mobiles, light fixtures, rugs.

Carton Doll's House

Needed: three (or four if preferred) *sturdy* cardboard cartons. Those shown (Fig. 49) are approximately 16½ by 11½ inches. For a roof use a heavy cardboard box opened out as shown, or two sides from other cartons, approximately 16 to 12 inches each, hinged at the peak if necessary with adhesive, masking or plastic tape. If four boxes are used, each roof section should be approximately 24 by 12 inches.

Fasten the boxes together with brass paper fasteners (indicated in Fig. 49 as small dots), punching holes with a bradawl, punch or nail. Attach roof in the same manner, but not until box tops are painted. Cut windows and doors with a heavy knife. Windows may be covered with cellophane if desired, then framed with ¼ inch width of white paper (see kitchen, Fig. 49).

Poster paint each room and the outside in the colours desired, beginning with the ceilings. The kitchen's

Crafts

"linoleum" floor is made by squeezing excess water from a sponge, dipping it into a colour contrasting to the floor colour, and pressing lightly in a regular pattern. Do not paint walls to be papered. Use border prints (see page 21), or scrap wallpaper, first using a small brush to coat the wall lightly with paste.

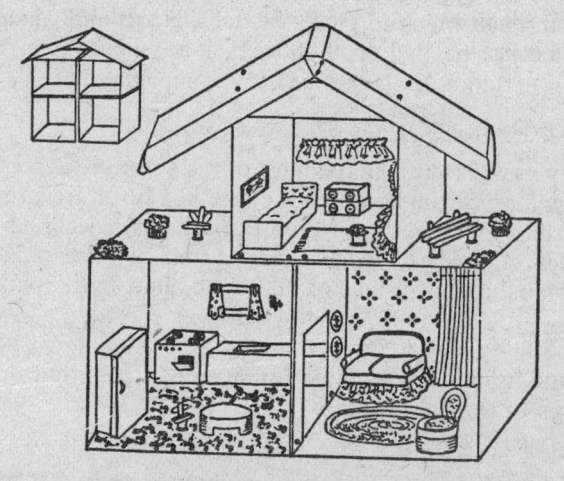

Fig. 49. Grocery-carton doll's house.

Kitchen: Refrigerator is a baby shoe-box with a twine handle knotted inside. Stove is a shoe-box cut in half. Sink unit is a long box with a hole cut the exact size of a smaller box, which is taped underneath for a sink. *Living room*: chair is the end of a round box, with a back cut from cardboard. Pillows for seat and back are glued on and match couch cover. *Bedroom*: Dressing table is made of a cream carton with pleated skirt, and cardboard kidney top glued on. Stool is a cotton reel with a bit of cotton covered by cloth tied with thread.

Make curtains (see page 60) and glue to the windows, as in the kitchen, or glue to a wall to cover a pretend-window, as in the living room, or gather on a string with brass fastenings to hold it, as in the bedroom. Make rugs (page 69) and glue lightly to the floors if desired.

Paint lower roofs green for balconies. Place small potted plants or bushes around and make a garden bench by gluing lollipop sticks to cotton reels as shown. (Lollipop sticks can be cut in half for back supports with heavy kitchen shears.)

Simplified Carton Doll's House

From the supermarket get a canned-goods carton that has the top cut around three sides only, making a hinged roof through which to place the dolls. Doors and windows may be just painted on. Follow shoe-box house (see page 55) or carton doll's house ideas for completing it.

Simplified Doll's House Rooms

If you wish to make the most of the furniture described below for a carton house, or the shoe-box furniture already described in "Shoe-Box House Furnishings", decorate the insides of several boxes, either carton or shoe size, as individual rooms instead of houses, to allow more space.

Doll's House Furniture

This furniture is suitable for supermarket carton doll's houses, or wooden houses.

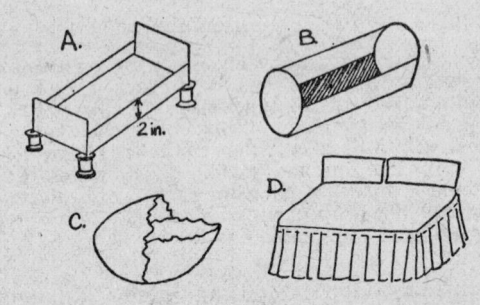

Fig. 50. (A) Shoe-box bed.
(B) Cradle.
(C) Eggshell cradle for one-inch doll.
(D) Studio couch.

BED: Glue four cotton reels to a baby's or child's shoe box for legs (Fig. 50, A). Cut away all but two inches of the

Crafts

sides. Cut away half of the footboard end. Leave the other end as it is for a headboard. Paint entire bed. Cover the headboard if desired with plastic or fabric. If a padded effect is wished, first glue a thin layer of cotton to the headboard.

For mattress and bedclothes, see "Shoe-Box House Furnishings".

CRADLE: Cut away half of the side of a small cylindrical box (Fig. 50, B) leaving ends as they are. Paint and decorate with ruffled netting, or cover with material glued on. Pad headboard as described under "Bed", above, if desired. Place a layer of thick cotton across the bottom before adding mattress and bedclothes (see "Shoe-Box House Furnishings). If desired one-third of the whole box may be left, to create a hooded top.

Variation: To make an eggshell cradle for miniature doll babies, break one egg in half lengthwise, one in half the usual way. Put one of the latter over one of the long halves (Fig. 50, C).

STUDIO COUCH: Turn a child's shoe-box upside down. Cover the bottom with a layer of cotton. Cut two pieces of material one inch larger all around than the box bottom. Lay one of these on the cotton padding, then glue down the sides, turning the corners neatly as with sheets on a bed, and gluing firmly.

Now cut a strip of the seat material 36 inches long and as wide as the box is deep. Glue or stitch pleats at regular intervals (see "Curtains", Fig. 51), and glue around three sides of the box (Fig. 50, D).

Go back to the second piece of material cut to match the seat. Cut this in half lengthwise. Fold each half and stitch inside out around three sides. Turn right side out, stuff with cotton or strips of nylon hose, stitch the end, and you will have two bolster pillows to prop at the back of the studio couch.

CHEST OF DRAWERS: Glue two or three large matchboxes

firmly together, one on top of the other. Paint with heavy poster paint or enamel. Glue a button or wooden bead to the middle of each, for a false drawer-pull. These boxes really can be used for drawers. (See doll's house bedroom, Fig. 48.)

SIDE TABLES: Cut away part of the sides of two sliders. Paint or cover with punch-dot mosaics.

COFFEE TABLE: For a rectangular table, follow side-table suggestions. If a long table is desired, place two boxes end to end. For a round table, use the bottom of a round box turned upside down and painted. If desired, part of the sides may be cut away. (See doll's house kitchen table, Fig. 48.)

COUCH: Turn a small shoe box upside down and make a couch seat and sides as for the studio couch (page 65). Cut a $2\frac{1}{2}$ inch-high piece of cardboard and fasten across the back with brass paper fasteners. Pad thickly with cotton, stretching it over the top. Make a cover, pillow-case style, leaving one of the long sides open, and allowing an inch larger than the cardboard back all around because of the cotton. Carefully slip over the back, gluing at the bottom.

PILLOWS: Use a drinking glass to draw outlines for two small circles of cloth. Stitch together wrong-side out, leaving an opening to insert cotton stuffing. Turn right-side-out, stuff, stitch opening. Sew a matching button exactly in the centre, pulling down tightly to cause the rest of the pillow to puff.

Make a 2 inch square pillow in similar fashion. If couch material is patterned, the pillows should be plain, for contrast.

BOOKCASES: Turn two or three large lidless matchboxes, or others of similar size, on their sides, and glue firmly together, making open shelves for books or knick-knacks. (To make books, see under "Shoe-Box House Furnishings".)

DINING TABLE: Use the bottom of a $3\frac{1}{2}$ inch-square jewellery

Crafts

box turned upside down. Break or cut four lollipop sticks to 3 inch lengths. Glue these, broken ends up, inside the four corners for legs. When dry, paint. (For a round, oatmeal-box type, see the doll's-house furniture, Fig. 48, E.)

CHAIRS: Follow suggestions given in "Shoe-Box House Furnishings". For the square table chair seats should be about 1½ inches high. Or use heavy kitchen scissors to cut 1-inch lengths of lollipop stick. Glue two lengths to a cotton reel Make backs as shown in doll's house, Fig. 48, D.

CURTAINS: For pull-back curtains, see "Shoe-Box House Furnishings". For informal curtains, cut strips of the material used for the couch, or use strips of netting, or old shirts or sheeting. Gather at the top and glue to both sides of the windows. A valance as described on page 61 may be used.

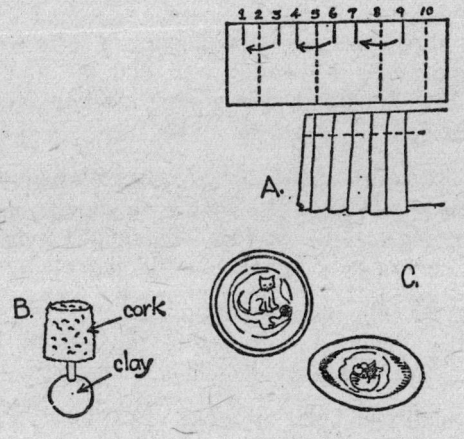

Fig. 51. (A) Method of pleating curtains.
(B) Lamp.
(C) Lid pictures.

For easy pleated curtains, cut a piece of material the length desired, and two and one-half times the width. Lightly pencil-mark every ½-inch as shown (Fig. 51, A), and fold line 3 to 1, line 6 to line 4, 9 to 7, and so on, stitching about ¼ inch from the top as you fold.

For informal curtain, leave pleats unpressed (doll's house furniture, Fig. 48, H). For formal "curtains" press pleats the entire length (doll's house bedroom) cut the length desired *plus* ½ inch and stitch a hem across the top. Run a string through this and fasten to brass fasteners at each end.

Doll curtains need not be hemmed, but if this is desired, add ½ inch to the length in cutting.

Doll's House Decorations

CENTREPIECE: Press a bit of heavy foil, or a doubled light piece, into a one-inch bowl. In this, place very tiny fruits of painted papier mâché or painted clay, for a table centrepiece. Or make a flat, rectangular dish of foil and "float" (without water, of course) tiny crêpe paper flowers (see page 33).

MIRRORS: For a dressing-table mirror, or for a wall ornament, use a round or oval lid from a cocoa tin or similar. This can be framed with tiny lace, or a small velvet ribbon can be glued on.

LAMPS: Use corks, painted or covered with material, with matchstick stems and a clay base wide enough to balance the lamp (Fig. 51, B). For standard lamps for a carton doll's house, use lollipop sticks and larger corks.

PICTURES: 1. Glue small pictures from a magazine or designs from material, or crayon drawings, inside aluminium milk-bottle caps, or small can lids (Fig. 51, C).

2. Cut small rectangles or circles of cardboard, rim with craft paper or rough material for a frame, and glue in a magazine picture or a crayon drawing.

Glue pictures to the doll's house walls in groups of two or more and about two inches from the floor.

PLANTS AND TREES: For indoor or terrace plants, make small pots of aluminium foil, soft-drink bottle caps, or corks

Crafts

Glue, tape or just push "greenery" into these depending on the type. The greenery can be sphagnum moss or lichen, crushed green tissue, or artificial Christmas greenery.

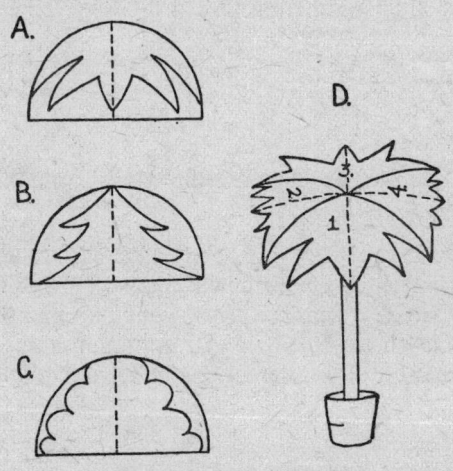

Fig. 52. Paper trees.

For a potted tree, use the lid of a wide-mouthed bottle. Cover with foil, fill with real soil or clay. Use a twig for a stem and a green top as for the potted plants.

For winter trees, use small-branched leafless twigs. Base in a small round of clay, papier mâché or plaster of Paris.

A paper tree can be made of green craft paper by cutting four 2-inch semi-circles, folding in half and then cutting these like a palm tree (Fig. 52, A), an evergreen (B), an oak (C), or any other. Glue the four semi-circles together at outer edges as in D. When dry glue the four-sided tree to a stick or twig, and make one of the bases or pot described above.

RUGS: Braid rugs (see page 91) to suit the rooms of the doll's house, or make woven paper mats. They may also be made of any scrap of material cut in the size or shape desired. The doll's house bedroom rug is a rectangle fringed by cutting in one inch on the ends.

70   555 Ways To Amuse Your Child

MOBILE: Make a miniature crossed-wire mobile and suspend miniature flowers from it.

LANTERNS: Miniature lanterns make charming modern light fixtures. Suspend from thread taped to the ceiling.

DOLLS

PIPE-CLEANER DOLLS: Here are directions for making three simple types:

1. The type shown in Fig. 53, A, takes two-and-a-half pipe-cleaner stems. One pipe-cleaner (B) forms the body and legs. One (C) forms the arms, wound around the centre to form the chest. One-half (D) is wound for the head. Cover with a bit of a different colour for a hat, glued on if necessary.

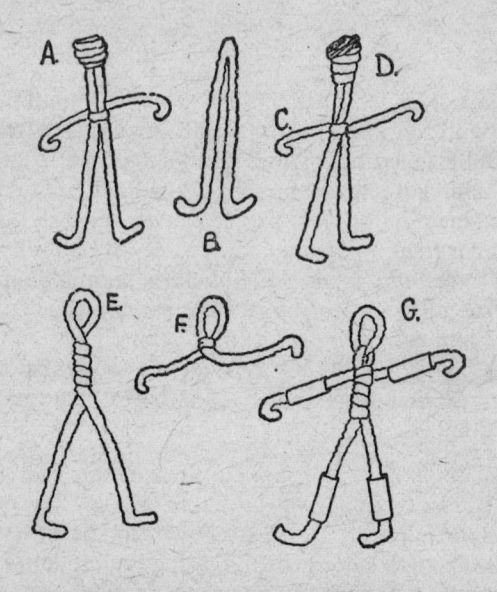

Fig. 53. Pipe-cleaner dolls.

Crafts

2. Begin as in (B) above. Twist, leaving a loop on top (E). Wind arms and head (F) through and around the loop left in (E). The finished figure (G) has drinking-straw bits covering arms and legs to make them seem more natural.

3. Make a figure as in (1) or (2) above, but double the length by joining two pipe-cleaners at the top, making a larger figure. If preferred, special long pipe-cleaners found in hobby shops, may be used, in which case one would be enough. Make a head of a bead, or attach a small polystyrene ball. Use sequins, beads, or hat pins for features. For hair use yarn, wool, thread, or a new wire pot cleaner.

ORNAMENTAL COTTON-REEL DOLL: A quaint little cotton-reel doll can be made with four large reels (Fig. 54, A). Paint three reels a pastel colour and glue together. Glue sequins, beads or glitter in a pattern.

Glue the unpainted reel on top, pencil in a face, then paint. Attach wool for hair by gluing one layer on top of another until desired thickness. Place a small paper flower or a sprig from an old artificial bouquet in the hair. Use as a gift or a dressing-table ornament.

FOIL DOLL: Lightly crush one piece of foil into the size and shape of a medium potato for the body. Crush another into a ball half that size for the head. Make twenty grape-size balls: four for each arm, five for each leg, one flattened ball for each foot. Wire all together (Fig. 54, B).

Make eyes and nose with beads or sequins held with hat pins. Use red nail enamel or a sliver of red tape for mouth. Give him a small cap of red crêpe or craft paper, or a pointed stocking cap made by twisting paper into a cone. Tie a bit of ribbon at the neck for a scarf, make buttons, and belt if desired, of red nail enamel, sellotape, sequins or felt.

Use for a Christmas ornament, a trinket gift or doll collection.

SOCK DOLL: Patterns for beatiful sock dolls may be bought, but the following one (Fig. 54, C) needs no pattern:

Choose a child's sock, size 8, perhaps red, with white

72　　　　　　　　　　　　　　　*555 Ways To Amuse Your Child*

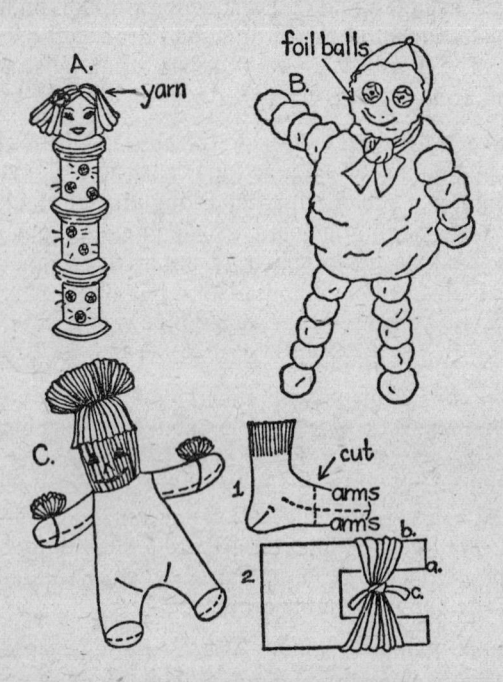

Fig. 54.　(A)　Cotton-reel doll.
　　　　　(B)　Foil doll.
　　　　　(C)　Sock doll.
　　　　　(C-1) Method of cutting sock.
　　　　　(C-2) Tassel on loom.

wool for trimming and black embroidery for features. Cut off half the foot, as shown in Fig. 54 (C-1) and cut this piece into two arms, stitching the sides and stuffing with cotton or small strips of old nylon stocking or tights, then stitching the tops closed.

Slit the remaining part of the foot to within 2 inches of the back of the heel, to form the legs. Turn inside out and stitch, closing "toes" and inside seam.

Stuff entire stocking up to 1½ inches from the top, where it must be tightly tied. Sew on the arms, tie the neck, embroider the face. Turn the top down for a hat. Stitch

Crafts

a small pompom (below) to the top and a very small one to each arm, at the "wrist".

TASSELS: For a head pompom for the doll above, or for doll clothes or doll curtains, make a 5-by-1 inch loom of heavy cardboard, cutting about a third out of the middle as shown in Fig. 54, C (2a). Wind a 3-yard strand of wool around the cut out end (b). Tie the centre (c), and gently remove from loom. Ends may be cut or not as desired. For a full-size tassel for dress or belt ties, clown pompoms, or pinning to curtains, make the loom 5-by-3 inches and use a 10 yard strand of wool. For the wrist tassels of the doll above, use a loom 5-by-½ inch width with 18 inches of wool.

TOYS OF PAPER AND PASTE

Boats

PAPER BOAT: The boat illustrated in Fig. 55 floats, and if made with waxed paper will last quite a while, but is too light for cargo, except possibly a small pipe-cleaner man.

Any size of paper may be used but must be square. An 8-by-8 inch square will make a boat about 6 inches long.

Fold to a triangle (Fig. 55, A, B). Fold point (1) to point (3), then point (2) to point (3) as shown in B. Carefully hold together the two half-flaps (1 and 2) with the *top* flap of (3), and fold back to (4). Now fold the remaining flap (3) back on the other side, making a triangle (C) that opens like a cone (D). Fold (5) and (6) together to make a small square (E). Turn the (5) and (6) section upside down and pull apart the flaps of (7), shown in F. This opens to the finished boat (G).

AMERICAN INDIAN WAR CANOE: Use a piece of craft paper 5-by-8 inches for an 8 inch canoe (Fig. 55 (bottom)). For a miniature canoe use a 3-by-4 inch sheet. Fold the paper lengthwise, then lightly in half the other way (A). Draw half of a canoe, cut out and unfold (B). Glue or tape the rounded ends together (1) to (2), (3) to (4). Hold apart at the centre

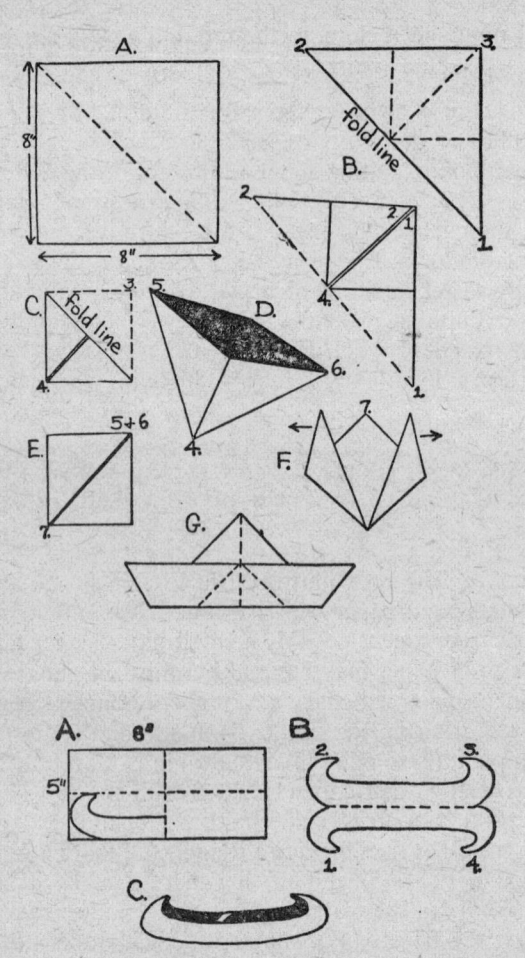

Fig. 55. (Above) Paper Boat.
(Below) American Indian War Canoe.

with a matchstick with the tip broken off (C). This also forms a seat.

WALNUT BOAT: Use a half shell of a walnut, or a split peach

Crafts 75

stone. Push a one-inch length of toothpick through a tiny triangle of paper, for a sail. Drop a blob of glue into the

Fig. 56. Walnut boat.

boat and prop sail in this until set, or use a very tiny ball of clay stuck fast (Fig. 56).

BOTTLE-CAP BOAT: Attach a sail (made as for the walnut boat above) to the cork inside a soft-drink bottle cap.

Fig. 57. Bottle-cap boat.

Traditional Circus Wagon

Paint a shoe-box with lid a bright colour. When dry cut openings in the sides, using a craft razor to provide the bars

Fig. 58. Traditional circus wagon.

for the cage (Fig. 58). On one end (the back of the wagon), cut a door to place animals in the cage. Use a brass paper fastener as a handle. Opposite it in the wall of the wagon, place a second fastener. Hold the door closed with a loop of thread or a rubber band stretched between the fasteners. Use a drinking-glass bottom or pair of compasses to draw circles, and cut wheels. Also cut a cardboard handle. Paint these a contrasting colour — yellow, perhaps, if the wagon is red. Attach wheels with brass fasteners. When finished, lid may be glued on if desired.

Suitcase

Tape one side of the lid of a shoe box to the bottom (1) as in Fig. 59, A, using a heavy tape such as plastic or adhesive. Tape the inside also by opening the lid fully when the outside is taped, and then taping the inside line. This is the hinged lid. If a sturdy box with lid attached can be found this step is saved.

On the suitcase front punch two small holes (2) and (3), as shown in B. Insert brass paper fasteners to close the suitcase, press finger under fastener (2) to permit closing.

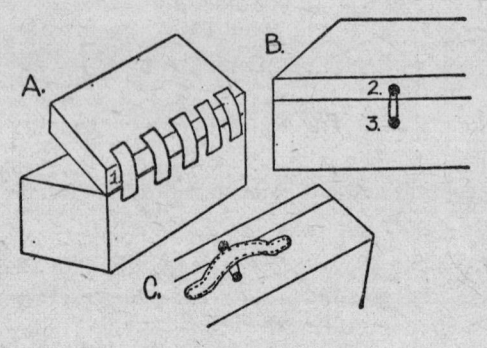

Fig. 59. Shoe-box suitcase.

To hold the suitcase closed, wind thin string around the two fasteners, unwind and place in the suitcase to prevent losing it when not in use. Strong rubber bands will hold the suitcase shut if preferred.

Crafts

For a handle, cut a piece of heavy cloth, 2-by-10 inches, fold lengthwise and stitch the three open sides under. Attach this to the suitcase front with two brass fasteners on each side for strength (C).

Piggy Bank

Find a cylindrical box. Cut a slit in the side of the box large enough for coins. The slit will be the top (Fig. 60).

Measure the length and circumference of the box. Cut a piece of paper this size. Use wrapping paper in a small all-over design. Cut two circles of the same paper the size of the round ends. Double another bit of the paper over and cut two double ears, gluing back and front together, or use gummed crêpe paper.

Fig. 60. Piggy bank.

Coat the sides of the box with glue and cover with paper, pressing out air holes; bring the ends together on the side opposite the slit. Cut the slit through the paper covering.

Glue the ears to the front circle of paper, and then glue it into position, pressing firmly. Curl the ears slightly with fingers or around a pencil or matchstick.

Glue on the back circle. Use a pencil to wind a pipe-cleaner for a tail, then push this through the back of the box. Make eyes of gummed paper hole reinforcements or circles of white paper. Cut the end from a large cork to shorten it, and paint it and four other corks, or cover with the paper. Cut two round circles of plain dark paper, or make with a paper punch, for nostrils. Glue nose and legs into position.

If you wish to be able to remove the money easily, cut a little door on the dotted lines as shown below the tail. Use a brass fastener for a handle, fasten another opposite it on the box, and run a loop of thread or a rubber band around both fasteners to hold door shut.

Stand-Up Animals

Colour, or cut from magazines bright animals and paste them on cardboard. Use spring clothes-pegs for legs (Fig. 61, A). They can be used as decorations for a party. Or

Fig. 61. Stand-up animals.

make small cardboard animals, give them stiff legs, with feet bent as shown, and use in the circus wagon (B).

Tent

Use khaki or green cloth if possible, although any scraps will do. Cut a rectangle 6-by-3½ inches. Cut a piece of cardboard 6-by-5 inches. Plastic-tape the long ends of the cloth to the long ends of the cardboard leaving a ¾ inch margin on each side. This gives the cloth enough leeway to place two toothpicks, one at either end, in the centre as tent poles (Fig. 62). Enough of the toothpick may be broken off to stand upright, blunt end up to prevent puncturing cloth.

Crafts 79

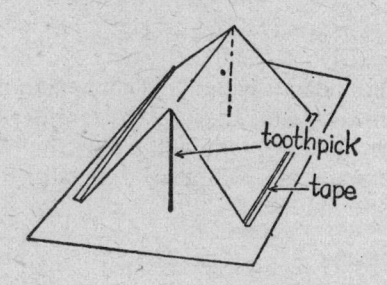

Fig. 62. Tent.

Use for battle games, camping, etc. To store, remove toothpicks and pack flat. (For another type of tent, see Fig. 41, page 54.)

Stretcher

For a stretcher for miniature men, use two straight twigs about $3\frac{1}{2}$ inches long. Toothpicks or matches will do but are a bit short. Glue a strip of cloth 3-by-$3\frac{1}{2}$ inches, to each twig, winding one full turn.

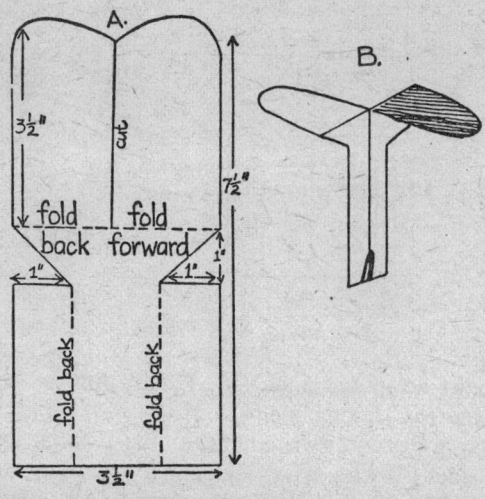

Fig. 63. Helicopter.

Helicopter

To make a whirlybird that flies, see Fig. 63. Use a 7½-by-3½ inch piece of heavy craft paper, and cut as shown (A). Fold wings as shown and fasten the lower folds with a paper clip, to give weight (B). Drop straight down from a height of four feet or more, and it will whirl as it falls.

Wallet

Fold an 8½-by-11 inch piece of paper in half (Fig. 64, A) along line (1). Then fold in the side borders (2) one inch each, resulting in B. Turn the top border on the unfolded

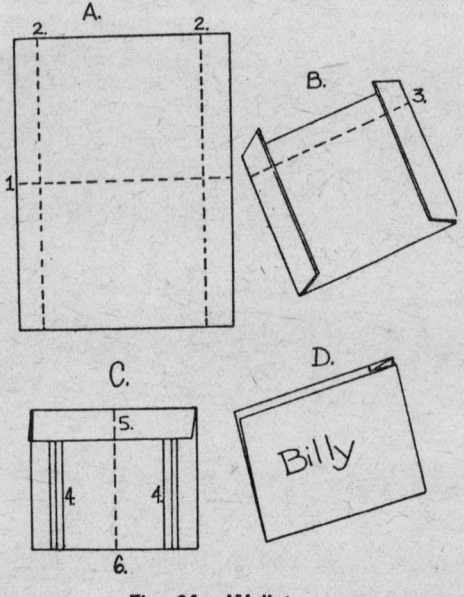

Fig. 64. Wallet.

edge (3) down one inch (B). Finally fold all this in half once more (C), along line (6).

Draw a design or write name on the outside. Seal flaps on both sides (4) with tape or glue. To open, lift flap (5). The result, D, is fine for play money, credit cards, etc.

Crafts

Train of Boxes

To make, use shoe boxes, small cartons from the shop, or matchboxes large or small, depending on the size train desired. Shoe shops sometimes have extra boxes they will give away.

ENGINE: To make a shoe-box engine, find two boxes, one just sufficiently smaller to fit snugly inside the other. For the cab, cut away about one third of the smaller box (Fig. 65, A). Cut holes in the sides for windows. Insert the larger section of the smaller box upright in the bigger box, with

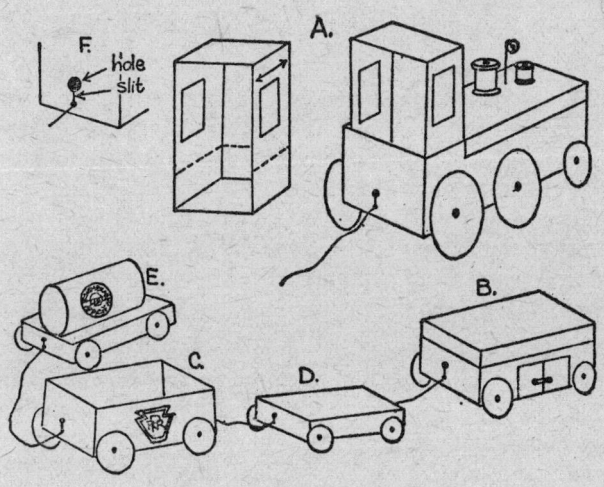

Fig. 65. Train of boxes.

open side facing back as shown. Attach a brass fastener in front of the large box for a headlight. Use drinking glasses for patterns, cut six discs from cardboard and attach with brass paper fasteners for wheels.

Now measure the depth of the cab box, as shown by the arrows in A, and cut away this amount from the large box lid. Glue or tape the lid to its own box, in front of the cab, as shown. Glue two cotton reels into position for funnels. Glue or tie two matchsticks together and tie on a small bell.

This engine is large enough to carry men, dolls, or animals. If wheels are not fastened too tightly, they will roll.

BOX CARS: Use boxes with lids for box cars (Fig. 65, B). Cut doors in the sides large enough to insert toys. To hold doors shut, use brass fasteners on the doors far enough apart to be held with a small rubber band.

GOODS TRUCKS: Lidless boxes (Fig. 65, C).

FLAT WAGGONS: The lids left over from the goods trucks (Fig. 65, D).

TANKERS: Cylindrical boxes glued to shoe-box lids (Fig. 65, E).

Tie cars and engine together with heavy string. To permit uncoupling, punch a small hole for the string. Cut a narrow slit from this hole up to another hole large enough to permit knot to slip through (Fig. 65, F).

To add more realism these can be painted with poster paints, but this should be done before assembling. Paint different names and symbols on the sides, similar to those on real trains.

MATCHBOX TRAINS: Either large or small sizes may be used. With these, turn the box upside down for the engine. Glue about one half of the slider to the top for the cab, after cutting out windows.

The large matchbox train is best for bed play.

African Native Hut

Measure the circumference of a brown paper bag, one that is around 18 inches or so. Cut a piece of corrugated packing paper (or other stiff paper) 3 inches high and as long as the bag is round, plus ½ inch for stapling.

Staple, plastic-tape or glue ends of corrugated paper together, rough side out and standing vertical as shown in Fig. 66, A, to resemble logs. Cut a door.

Cut the bottom from the brown bag, leaving a cylinder

about 7 inches high. Bend the top of the corrugated cylinder inward and glue the bag to the base, permitting the bag to overhang the edge about an inch (B).

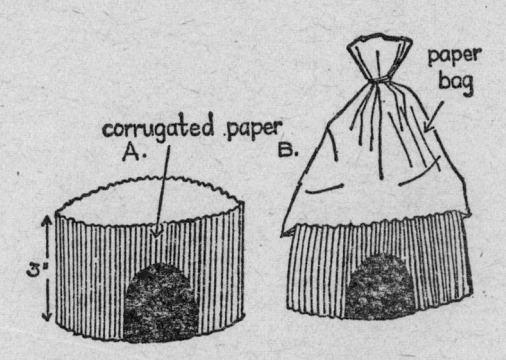

Fig. 66. African native hut.

Squeeze in the top and hold with tape or string. Make several for games with wild animals and natives, or make a miniature size for an African miniature scene.

Grocery-Carton Separators

Boxes sometimes contain corrugated separators to protect jars or bottles. These can often be obtained from off-licences or supermarkets. Here are several uses:

1. Stand on one end for a doll cupboard. Paint if desired. If necessary, tape to the wall of the doll's house to hold upright. If too large, cut *between* the separators (see dotted lines, Fig. 67) to prevent it falling apart.

2. Stand on one side to create an apartment house for miniature dolls. Tape to a side of the carton it came in, or the box itself, to prevent falling.

3. Use as an aviary (home for birds) by turning on its side and following directions in (2). Make miniature birds following the patterns in Figs. 26 and 27. Attach birds to a string and tape the string to the top of each section for individual cages. Add this to a zoo.

4. Cut the depth of the separators in half along broken lines as shown (Fig. 67). This will create small pens for a zoo or stockyard, or low dividers for a hobby collection.

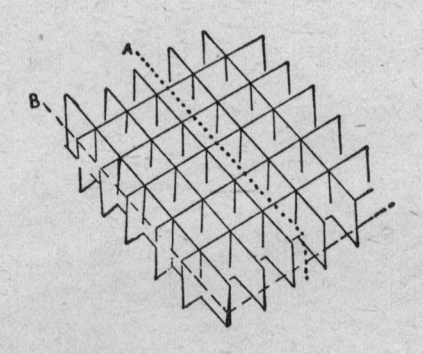

Fig. 67. Grocery carton separators.

5. Cut on dotted lines, and then along broken lines, to fit a small box or drawer. Use as a separator for jewellery, combs, small toys, trinkets.

Enclosures, Fences, Stone Walls

Cut with scissors or slice off with a heavy knife, 2-inch-deep, unbroken sections from a small grocery carton, as

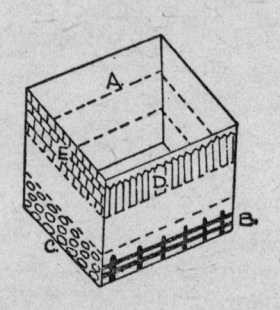

Fig. 68. Enclosures, fences and walls made from a grocery carton.

Crafts　　　　　　　　　　　　　　　　　　　　　　　　85

shown in Fig. 68, A. Use as enclosures, zoo pens, yard or field fences or walls. For more realism, pencil in a design (below), and paint or colour before cutting.

To make "logs", stroke up and down with brown paint, first a light stroke, then a dark. For railings, paint the background lightly if necessary to cover advertising, and the rails as shown (B). For a stone wall, paint grey, brown or white markings (C). For a pointed stake fence, paint in white stripes and point at the top (D). For a brick wall, paint red, with white lines for bricks (E).

Log Cabins

To make, use corrugated packing paper with the rough side out and running horizontally to resemble logs. Either a tiny one for a miniature scene, or a shoe-box size for a village can be made the same way.

First, cut two rectangles, about 9 by 4 inches (Fig. 69, A).

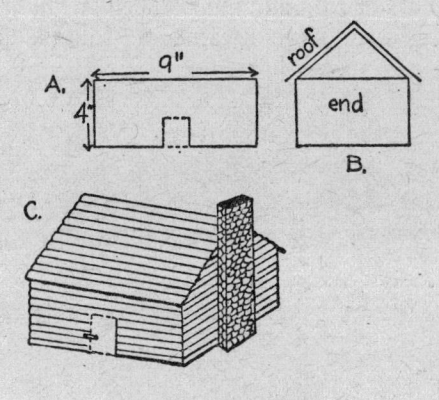

Fig. 69. Log cabin.

Cut two ends 6 inches wide by 4 inches high, but with a peaked top (B). Lay one on top of the other to match exactly. Cut a door along the dotted lines (A). Use a brass paper fastener for a handle. Use a craft razor to cut a window in one end piece.

Glue or plastic-tape the sides together. For the floor, cut

a piece of carton 7 by 10 inches. Make lines on the plain side to resemble floorboards. Set up walls on floor and tape together around the inside.

Cut a roof 11 inches wide and 2 inches longer than distance around the triangular peak (B), to create eaves on both sides. Be sure the "logs" run across the paper, not lengthwise. Crease in the centre for the ridge; glue into position. Use a light weight if necessary and allow a whole day to dry.

For a chimney, cut two 7 by 1 inch strips and two 7 by $\frac{1}{2}$ inch strips of grey or white cardboard. Draw lines as shown to resemble stones. Tape three sides together on the inside, tape the fourth side, and glue or plastic-tape to windowless end.

To use the cabin with miniature men, the back wall may be omitted, or just propped into position.

Experiment with matchstick or toothpick cabins, or twig-and-mud or rock-and-mud cabins. For these make the roof by covering a piece of cardboard with the "logs".

2
HOBBIES

While hobbies are special interests which give pleasure in spare time, they also have a real value for a young person. Some hobbies, such as history, science or nature, may lead to adult vocations. Others, such as art, music or stamp-collecting, may lead to lifetime enrichment. Hobbies provide a means of exploring the world.

There are various ways to add to the value of a hobby, but any of them become more fun when shared with another who has the same interest.

WAYS TO BUILD UP A HOBBY

Collecting

There are a number of special fields that can be *collected*: shells, rocks and other nature items, traditional handicrafts, coins, stamps, dolls and others.

A collection will be more interesting if kept together in a box or drawer. And it will mean more if it is *labelled*. When a rock is found and discovered to be granite, it should be labelled before the name is forgotten. And the collection will be most interesting of all if *mounted* or *sorted*

SUGGESTED METHODS:

1. Plaster of Paris.

2. In special boxes with separators — egg cartons, for example. (To make a box, see "Grocery-Carton Separators", page 83.)

3. Glued to boards, or stiff cardboard such as the side of a grocery carton.

Scrapbook

This is particularly useful for building up a hobby that cannot be collected, such as outer space and the atom. A scrapbook can add to a collecting hobby by recording information found in magazines and newspapers, and notes from reading on the subject. It can include sketches made in the field, pictures from magazines, photographs.

A scrapbook can include also special crafts such as ink prints for leaves, flowers, spatter prints, designs.

Interest may be added to a scrapbook by including poetry on the subject chosen, and by arranging pictures and information artistically. Do not crowd too much on a page, and balance one large picture with several small.

The value of the scrapbook will be greatly increased if material is not pasted in until several pages are ready (unless it is loose-leaf), so that information on the same phase of the subject may be placed together. Keep materials in a file or envelope until ready.

Research

Build up a hobby interest through research. Read about the subject in library books, ask for a gift of one or two of the best for reference.

Make full use of the senses to *observe* — especially in the world of nature. Eyes trained to see the flitting of a bird in the bush, the dewy web of a spider in the early morn, will find not only more knowledge but more beauty.

And finally, an important part of research: experiment. Read, observe, and then, experiment. If a microscope is available, chip off a bit of rock to examine. Use a magnifying glass to study stamps. Compare the growth of a bean seed to that of a pea. Many hobbies offer a first-rate chance to see what makes the world work.

Craft Work

Another way to build up a hobby is in the use of craft

work. Model animals for an animal hobby in clay or papier mâché, or carve them in soap. Sketch or paint birds for a bird collection, with a drawing of nest and egg beside each.

Even someone with little artistic ability can copy from books and magazines. A scrapbook on butterflies would profit from pictures drawn by looking at copies in books.

Related Activities

A last way to build up a hobby is to do things related to the hobby. Travel will nearly always teach more about many hobbies, especially history, geography, nature, foreigners. All areas, including your own, have museums and natural beauty spots and places of historic interest to investigate. Often there are musical records about a chosen subject, or films, or special shops that deal in the materials needed.

AEROPLANES AND JETS

Make a scrapbook of planes. Build plastic models, which can be hung from mobiles in your room. Visit airports and museums. Read some of the many books on the subject, both fact and fiction.

ART

Drawing, painting and sculpturing are not only wonderful hobbies in themselves; they also provide doors to other hobbies. If history is a special interest, study art from the drawings of primitive man to the present. If you are a nature lover, keep a sketch pad handy when outdoors, or a plastic bag of clay in your pocket, to sketch or mould what you see. If you find people absorbing, sketch their faces. Visit the art exhibits in museums, keep a scrapbook of magazine reproductions of great masterpieces.

BRAIDING

Stitch or knot three strands of material together (Fig. 70, A) Pin to a box, bedspread or other sturdy surface, to make the work go rapidly until a good start has been made.

First, pull the right strand (1) in front of the middle strand (2) as in B. Now pull the left strand (3) in front of the present middle strand (1), which was originally the right

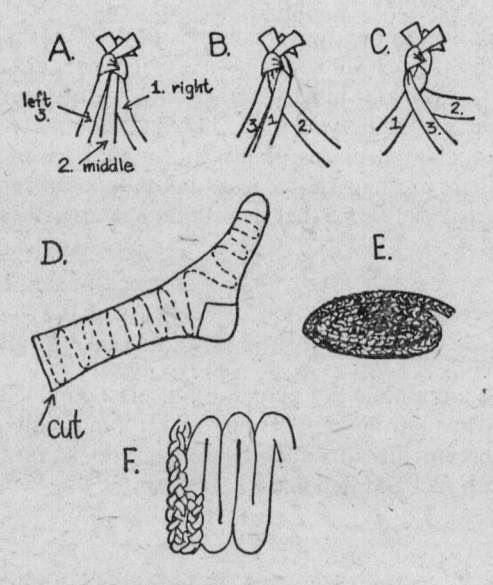

Fig. 70. (A-C) Method of braiding.
(D) A sock cut for braiding.
(E) Round or oval rug.
(F) Rectangular rug.

strand, as in C. This is the entire process of braiding: constantly pulling first the right strand, then the left strand, over the middle strand. Pull just tightly enough to make a neat, even braid.

When stopping work, loosely knot the ends of the strands to prevent unravelling until complete. When finished, stitch or knot strands together.

Braided Rug

Save all the bright, attractive socks that are to be discarded. Either nylon socks or cotton will do, but it is better not to mix them. Choose colours to suit the room for which the rug is intended. Cut off the elastic band at the top. Begin cutting a long, winding strand that need not be broken until the toe is reached (Fig 70, D). You will find the heel can be cut away entirely without breaking the strand. If the foot is stained or mended, the strand can end at the heel. It can then be kept as it is or cut into workable lengths if too long.

For a room rug, cut stocking strips ½-inch wide. For a doll's rug, cut ¼-inch strips. In working, as the end of each strip of material is reached, stitch a new strand to the one in use.

To make the rug, braid several feet, then begin at the centre for a round rug (E). Wind one row against the next, as shown, sewing firmly with a strong thread, braiding ahead several feet each time as you work. To avoid buckling do not sew too tight. Knot the sewing thread at frequent intervals to prevent unravelling in the wash.

For a rectangular rug, begin at one end (F).

CARS AND TRUCKS

Keep a scrapbook of the development of cars and trucks from an earlier day. Learn to recognise the various models on the road. Watch when an engine is being repaired and ask questions if permissible. Learn the purpose of each object on the dashboard. Buy and build the inexpensive cast models, or make a toy car collection.

COINS

Begin by saving one new coin from each denomination: 1p, 2p, 5p, 10p, etc. Check the family purses regularly for older coins now going out of circulation: shillings, two shilling pieces, etc. Keep several of each for swopping purposes, and replace worn coins with newer ones where possible.

Ask older friends and relatives for coins now out of date. Ask travelling friends to bring back coins from other countries.

Keep the collection in flannel, or small transparent plastic envelopes, to avoid rubbing. Separate the coins by countries, keeping Italian money separate from British money, and so on.

Visit a numismatic shop to see unusual coins.

COOKING

Cooking can be an absorbing hobby even to boys and men. Prepare very simple foods until you feel at home in the kitchen. Keep a card file of favourite recipes.

Here are a few ideas to begin on: cinnamon toast, hot dogs, hamburgers, welsh rarebits, gingerbread men, sweet biscuits.

(See also "Camping", Chapter 6, for camp cooking, and "Foods", Chapter 3.)

DOLLS

Many girls collect dolls, but few have a collection of *home-made* dolls. They can be made of clay, papier mâché, or play dough; of beads, cotton reels, yarn, foil, clothes pegs, nature items such as cones or shells. (See also "Houses and Dolls", Chapter 1.)

FLOWER ARRANGING

Study flower arrangement in books and magazines, and make a scrapbook of clever ideas. Visit flower displays at fêtes and horticultural shows. Experiment with materials from your own garden.

Hobbies

Here are a few general rules on flower arrangement :

1. Use as few flowers as possible to permit each to stand out clearly.

2. Bouquets are most frequently in a triangular shape, narrow at top, extending out and down.

3. Put larger, heavier flowers near the base.

4. Have stems cut to various lengths. Pull off leaves below the water line to lengthen the life of the bouquet.

5. Pick colours that match, harmonise or contrast with the room. If the living room is pink, save the orange roses for the yellow kitchen.

Here are a few arrangements for beginners to try :

1. Use one, two or three flowers in a slim vase. Balance with leaves.

2. Float one, two or three flowers in a bowl, separated by floating leaves. This is especially good for flowers that do not last well otherwise, or those with stems that cannot be cut, such as camellias. Try roses, dahlias, gardenias.

3. Add a colourful rock or piece of deadwood or a small figurine to your arrangement. Or stand in front of a small screen (such as a thin bamboo mat stood on end). Or make or buy a wooden base to suit vase or bowl.

4. Collect, and arrange attractively, nature items such as dried seed pods, rocks, cones, moss, and so on. Use deadwood and driftwood. Experiment with courgettes, dried sweetcorn, preserved leaves, nuts, etc. Place figurines nearby, such as pheasants.

Create small scenes — wood with animals, evergreens with cotton-wool for snow, candle figures set in evergreen, etc.

GARDENING

Outdoor

Have the soil prepared in advance, and follow packet directions telling how deep and far apart to plant. Vegetables are fast-growing. Try radishes, onions, French beans, stick beans, peas, tomatoes, leeks, cauliflowers.

The best flowers for children to grow are annuals, which must be replanted every year but grow quite fast. Try marigolds and others suggested by a local shop for showy beauty and rapid growth. Most annuals are planted in the spring. Flowers from seed are grown more easily if started in seed trays indoors (see below).

Bulbs also are easily grown. These can be "forced" indoors (see below), or planted deep outdoors in the autumn. Follow packet instructions for depth, place and time. These should not be planted in a row but grouped, three or four together, for bright spots of early colour here and there in the garden. If planted at intervals throughout the autumn the colour will last longer.

Indoor

FORCING BULBS: For bright, long-lasting indoor colour that requires no arranging, plant narcissus. Fill a pretty, low dish with water and sand, shells or gravel; place in it two or three bulbs. In a week start two or three more, and so on for continuous indoor bloom.

FORCING BRANCHES: Cut short branches from deciduous trees in late winter, place in water and await results. Fruit trees and pussy willows are especially rewarding.

SEED TRAYS: Start flower seeds in small containers, to protect them from frost and give them a good start. If more than one type is planted, identify by writing name of plant on a lollipop stick and pushing it into the earth.

Old ice cream containers are excellent for trays. Remove top. Fill about half full with topsoil, mixed with peat moss if available. Make two small furrows with a stick, and plant the seed about 1½ inches apart, following packet directions for depth. Keep the soil moist. When plants are 2 or 3 inches high and sturdy, transplant outdoors. Use a trowel and be careful to remove the surrounding soil with the plant to avoid shock to the roots. Have the new planting ground prepared ahead of time.

EXPERIMENTS: It is not necessary to dig up seeds outdoors to see how the garden is getting along. Instead, try the following:

1. Make an ice cream tray (see above), and mark it off into fourteen small squares by laying string on the earth or drawing lines with a stick. The day you plant your seed outdoors, plant *one* of the same in the centre of a corner square. Insert a lollipop stick in the same square giving date. On the next day plant another of the same seeds in the next square, again labelling the day. (The day can be taped or scratched into the side of the box if preferred.) Then, each day for two weeks, plant one more seed. If the outdoor plants are not up by this time, mark off another tray and continue with one daily seed-planting until the outdoor plants are above an inch high.

When the outdoor plants are up, carefully uproot the tray samples, working in order of the planting, to get a picture of the day-by-day development of seed-into-plant. Beans or peas are excellent for this experiment.

2. Plant a variety of seeds in ice cream trays. These should be two inches apart. Try apple seeds, acorns, conkers, uncooked prunes. When walking pick up seeds in wild areas or along park footpaths. Label each seed with the name, if possible, and date of planting. Be sure to keep the soil damp.

3. For a short-term experiment, to watch seeds germinating from seed into plant, place fast-sprouting seeds such as beans or peas in a glass jar. Have the jar lined with damp blotting paper curved inside, and drop the seeds between jar and liner. Keep blotting paper moist.

4. To prove that seeds reach for light and heat, plant a seed in a closed box. Cut a pen-sized hole well away from the seed. The lid must be movable to permit watering, and the soil should be kept moist.

Watch the results, and you will discover that seeds, with no guiding eyes, always grow up toward the world instead of deeper into the soil.

GEOGRAPHY

One of the best ways to learn of places is to study maps. Whenever there is mention of a certain place on TV or in books or conversation, look it up in the atlas or on a globe. Use wall-board panels to display a world map and one of Great Britain, perhaps in a hall.

Make a collection of maps. Keep a scrapbook of places of especial interest to you. Travel of course is ideal for a geography hobby, but reading is satisfying too. (See "Geography", Chapter 3.)

HISTORY AND ARCHAEOLOGY

History, the story of man's past, and biography the stories of the men who made that history, form an interesting hobby. Add archaeology, the study of the cities and objects earlier civilisations have left behind, to broaden an understanding of the past.

There is a world of books in these fields. There are colourful magazine advertisements telling one special story, suitable for a scrapbook collection. There are museums and historical places to visit wherever you travel.

Read historical fiction and then look up the background in the encyclopedia. In this field try the many books on prehistoric times, the Roman Conquest, and the Middle Ages. Read biographies of the great scientists discoverers, and leaders in thought, Government and art.

HOME DECORATING

Make a scrapbook of magazine pictures showing rooms that attract you. Learn to observe unusual homes you visit, and note professional decorating tricks in show houses. Try to discover the reasons for their appeal.

Home Decorating Ideas

1. Pictures and wall ornaments should be at eye level. Small items seem more important in pairs or grouped.

2. Choose three or four colours for a room and try to hold to these. You might choose pink and green, for example, with touches of grey and white. Experiment with a doll's house and furniture.

3. Balance figured surfaces with plain. Too many designs are confusing to the eye.

4. Avoid clutter. Dressers, tables, headboards should be bare except for a very few decorative items. Change these to add interest and prevent tiring of your treasures. If no tablecloth is used, glue bits of felt or polystyrene to the bottoms of vases, jewel boxes, etc., to protect furniture.

5. Suit the decoration to the room: woody arrangements in rustic rooms; shells in rooms with a tropical motif or in the bathroom, adding fish net, baskets, ceramic mermaids, and fish, etc.

KNOT TYING

The cow hitch is one of the most practical knots. Use it to fasten items to a belt, leaving the hands free, or for yarn fringe:

Use a double rope, as shown (Fig. 71, A), or a single rope or string doubled back. The centre loop in this case (B) is pulled up from behind the belt, yarn hole or other

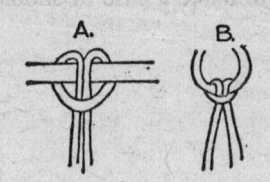

Fig. 71. Cow hitch, a knot of many uses.

object. The loop is held open while the ends are pulled through it from the front, then closed by pulling end taut.

LEATHERWORK

Leather or hobby shops sell inexpensive scrap leather. Leatherwork also requires lacing, and a leather punch. The cheapest type of punch resembles a pencil with a hole where the point should be. Pound on an old board to prevent blunting.

Always draw a pattern for leatherwork first on paper and use this for a guide.

Leather Thongs

Many crafts call for leather thongs for lacing or tying, but the straight edges of the scrap leather, which have so many uses, need not be wasted on these. Use any odd shape, cutting continuously around the edge in a thin strip until the necessary length is reached.

PETS

Animal lovers will find pets an interesting hobby if permissible. Make a scrapbook of pets and information concerning them. Read books about animals.

PHOTOGRAPHY

This is an expensive hobby, so begin with a small, cheap

Hobbies 99

camera. It is wise to make a case or shoulder bag for it, or at least to wear it on a string around the neck when on a trip. Also attach a band of adhesive tape to camera carrying name, address and telephone number.

Study each group of pictures to see what is wrong. If information is sent by the developing company, read it carefully. It is cheaper and more fun to learn to develop prints at home.

Keep pictures together in an album. Even a loose-leaf notebook will do if necessary, with photo tabs used to hold the pictures and permit later removal. File them until ready to arrange in an album. Label lightly on the back with names, dates and places. Transfer this information to a strip of white paper to be glued beneath the picture, or write it under the picture.

PREHISTORIC TIMES

Build a collection of prehistoric monsters and cave people, for use in games. Use them to build miniature scenes in a grocery carton, or for a home museum display. Visit museums for prehistoric displays.

SEWING

Sewing can be the most useful of hobbies. Following are simple beginners' items.

Felt Belt

Cut a 2-inch strip of felt, one inch shorter in length than your waist. On the last 2 inches on each end, stitch a piece of thin leather or heavy material underneath to strengthen the felt. The thread should match the felt. On each end punch or cut three ⅛-inch holes in a row (Fig. 72). Use leather thong or ribbon to lace through the holes for a tie. Decorate the felt by gluing to it tiny bits of contrasting

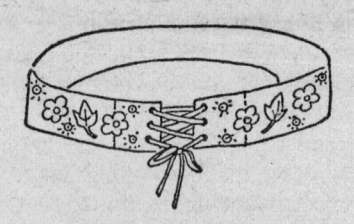

Fig. 72. Felt belt.

colours of felt cut in geometric figures, toy shapes, or dolls. Or stitch sequins or beads to the belt in a pattern.

Fun Tie

Buy one yard of one-inch-wide satin or ribbed ribbon in a pretty pattern and colour. Knot loosely around the neck to measure for length, and cut if necessary. Neatly hand-

Fig. 73. Fun tie.

stitch the two ends to prevent fraying, and then decorate with sequins or beads, using initials, circles, lines, etc. Learn to tie a man's tie knot. Wear with blouses or give as a gift (Fig. 73).

Elf Bag

This requires a 12-by-13 inch piece of felt. For a girl's purse cut a 12-inch square of felt leaving a thin strip along

Hobbies

the side; make a 6-inch square for a doll's, with all other measurements half-size too.

Fold the 12-inch square as shown (Fig. 74, A), stitching the numbered seams together $3\frac{1}{2}$ inches toward the centre,

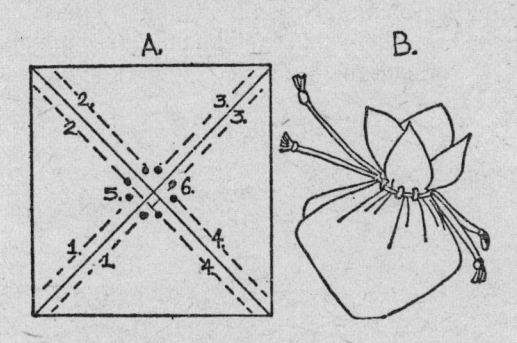

Fig. 74. Elf bag for girl or doll.

(1) to (1), (2) to (2), and so on. Turn the other side out, and sew on curtain rings or felt strips as shown by the dots (A). This is the basic purse.

Now use the leftover strip to cut two handles, each 12-by-$\frac{1}{2}$ inch. Loop one through each ring, beginning and ending at (5), tying tightly and then fringing the handle edge beyond the knot. Now loop the second handle, beginning and ending at (6). Pull up cords and the elf bag is done (B).

Cushions

Cut the 13-inch square basic cushion case from an unworn section of old sheeting, unbleached muslin, etc., folded double. Turn wrong side out and machine-stitch three sides. Turn right side out and fill with feathers or padding. Turn the edges of the fourth side in and machine-stitch.

For a round cushion, cut two circles 13 inches across, using a plate for a pattern if you have no compasses. Stitch together, leaving about one third open for filling.

The cushion cover is made in the same manner except that it is 14 inches across, and the fourth side is hand-stitched for removal of the cover for washing.

102   555 Ways To Amuse Your Child

To decorate:

1. Quilt a cover

2. Draw simple designs or get them from other sources (Fig. 75, A), tracing them on to a 14-inch square or circle of bleached muslin or other solid-colour or white material. Outline the designs in a simple embroidery stitch in colours to suit the room.

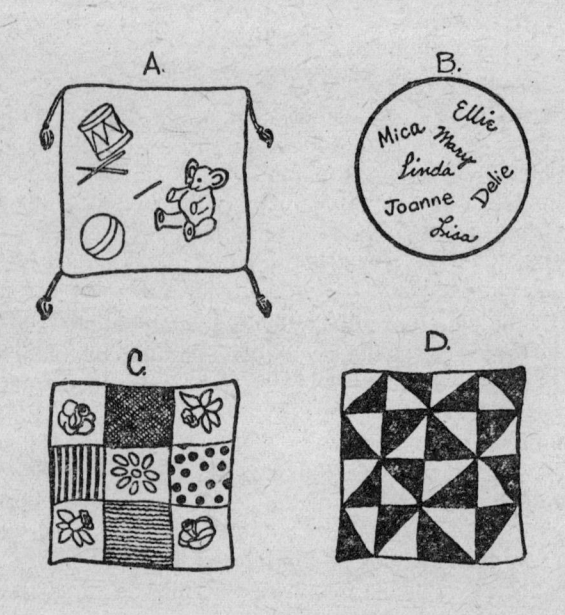

Fig. 75. Cushions to make.

(A) Embroidered designs.
(B) Signature cushion
(C) Combined quilting and embroidery.
(D) All-over quilted pattern.

3. Ask friends to write their names, in pencil and rather large writing, on the cushion-cover material. Embroider each in a different colour, or all in one colour (B).

4. Combine quilt and embroidery patterns by making every other square plain white, with a design or a signature embroidered on the white. The alternate squares will be of various materials (C).

5. Make a cushion cover of the curtain material of the room.

The plainer cushions, such as the signature case, can be brightened with an edging of washable and prewashed curtain fringe, with a row of quilting or with tassels tied to the corners.

Quilting

Piecing a quilt is the process of cutting leftover scraps of new cloth into shapes, and stitching these together in a pattern, to form a whole cloth.

To quilt some cushions for a room, first make the basic cushion. Cut several pretty, washable materials into shapes that will fit well together, such as triangles, diamonds, squares, long bars or hexagons.

Lay the patterns out in a pleasing combination. Patterned areas are more attractive when separated by plain (Fig. 75, D). Stitch pieces together, making the quilted front one inch larger all around than the basic cushion will be. Stitch three edges, wrong side out, to a back of sheeting or bleached muslin; turn right side out, put basic cushion inside and hem the fourth edge by hand to permit removal for washing.

Sewing Stitches

The sewing stitches pictured in Fig. 76 are the most basic stitches used: blanket stitch (A), tacking stitch (B), buttonhole stitch (C), chain stitch (D), solid embroidery (E), embroidered running or outline stitch (F). To make a French knot, push needle into cloth, wind thread around needle three times, and pull thread through for finished knot.

104   555 Ways To Amuse Your Child

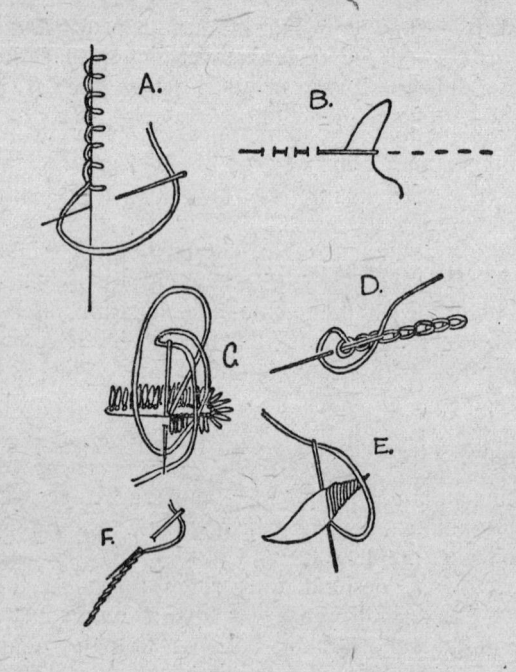

Fig. 76. Sewing stitches.
(A) Blanket stitch.
(B) Tacking stitch.
(C) Buttonhole stitch.
(D) Chain stitch.
(E) Solid embroidery.
(F) Embroidered running or outline stitch.

How to Fringe

1. On material that doesn't unravel, fringe can be made by cutting at intervals the entire distance, as in Fig. 77, A.

2. The most common type of fringe, used for stoles and rug edges, is made with the cow hitch (B). (See "Knot Tying" on page 97 for instructions.)

3. Diamond pattern (C): this is an elaboration of the fringe, above, using the cow hitch.

Hobbies 105

Loop-tie (with a cow hitch) six strands of wool or string through each hole. Divide each bundle of strands into two bundles of three each. Leave the end three loose. Take the last three strands of the first loop and tie to the first three

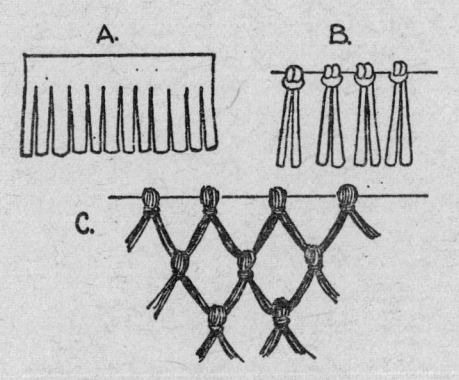

Fig. 77. Methods of fringing.

strands of the second loop by winding the combined bundle of six around the finger and knotting, as shown. Take the second three strands of the second loop and the first three strands of the third and knot, and so on across the row.

A second row of ties, to form the diamond, is made in the same manner as shown.

4. Pull fringe: use for card-table or doll's-table covers, napkins, table mats. This is easiest with materials that unravel easily and have a rather coarse weave.

Remove all selvedge. Loosen with pin or fingernail the last thread of the cut edge of material. Pull gently until it comes away from the material. Continue, thread by thread, until the desired amount of fringe has been created.

If materials with this fringe are shaken while damp, they can be ironed more easily. Gently run a clean comb through to straighten knotted fringe.

Laundry-Bag Doll

Cut two circles 18 inches in diameter of checked gingham

or other material. Cut a slit in one, to the centre of the circle, hemming each side (Fig. 78, A). Stitch circles together, inside out, leaving two 3-inch openings at the bottom (B), and a 6-inch opening at the top. When right side out, insert two flaps of white felt, or other washable material in bottom openings and stitch tight for doll's shoes (see finished bag, Fig. 78). Turn the 6-inch opening under the hem (C). Also run a heavy tacking thread around this opening

Use the toe of a new, white, man's sock for a head. Stuff the toe with old nylon stocking strips and hem just ahead of the heel. Create a face with embroidered thread or buttons. Add wool hair. To the top of the head attach firmly a loop of doubled material stitched together for a handle to hang on a wall.

Fig. 78. Laundry-bag doll.

Now insert the head in the 6-inch opening, draw the tacking thread tight and stitch the "body" to the head very firmly, before removing tackings.

Stuff the doll with soiled hosiery or other small laundry items by inserting in the front slit.

Travel Shoe Bags

Lay a man's shoe on two thicknesses of cloth. Mark a rectangle two inches larger than the shoe all the way around,

Hobbies

and cut. Machine-stitch around three sides, leaving two inches of the last side unstitched as shown (Fig. 79). Fold the open end down one inch and hem. Be sure to leave open one end of the hem. Through this run a string from old pyjamas,

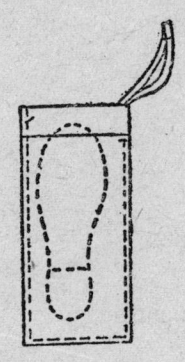

Fig. 79. Travel shoe bag.

or mending tape. Stitch ends of string together to prevent slipping out.

Make two of these for each pair of shoes. Use in suitcases to prevent shoes from soiling clothes. Shoe bags make excellent gifts.

SHIPS

Build or buy small models in bottles, etc. Build plastic models of famous ships. Make a scrapbook of pictures and news stories about them. Boys may find a Sea Scout troop near their home.

Read stories of the sea, the Navy and pirates. When visiting harbour towns, investigate chances to board Navy ships, fishing boats, or historic ships.

STAMPS

Stamp collecting can be the most expensive of hobbies,

but a fine collection that will give much pleasure can be built up with very little cost.

Some collectors save cancellations and postmarks as well and cut out the entire corner. Some soak stamps from letters. Some save only new stamps, in units of four. An amateur can suit himself, but it is wise to save several of each for swopping purposes.

Remove stamps from old envelopes. Check the post office regularly for new issues.

Keep stamps sorted by country and boxed until ready to mount them. Albums can be purchased for this purpose, but beginners usually have more fun using plain white paper in a loose-leaf book, mounting the stamps with stamp hinges. This permits later removal without damage if desired. Keep all of one country together. With British stamps, sort by denominaiton: 10p, 20p and so on.

TRAINS

Build up a toy train collection. Make plastic or cardboard models of real trains. Visit locomotive collections, museums and private steam railways when possible, especially when travelling.

WEAVING

The principles of weaving, given below, may be adapted to many other objects, such as doll rugs, or wall "tapestries" for doll houses.

Round Purse

Cut two discs of heavy cardboard 6 or 8 inches in diameter, depending on the size purse you wish. Use a pair of compasses or small plate bottom for a pattern. With a ruler and pencil, mark each disc in halves, then quarters, etc., until there are sixteen lines. Readjust three or four of them as shown (Fig. 80, A) to make room for a seventeenth line,

Hobbies

and notch edges about ¼ inch deep as shown. Each disc forms a loom for half the purse.

Paste the end of a piece of wool over the centre of the loom. When dry, start at the centre and wind the wool out back to the centre (3), on across to (4-5-6), and so on until the wool has been pulled through each notch, ending in the centre. The last strand from notch to centre will double, but is handled as if it were single.

Now you have your warp. Fasten the weaving yarn to the centre, run the end through a large blunt needle and

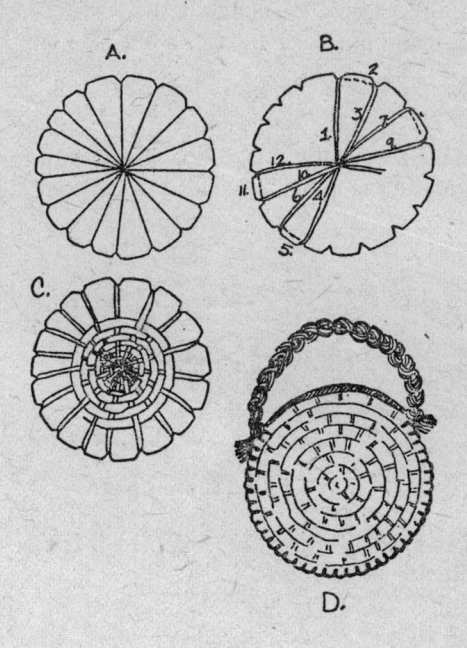

Fig. 80. Woven purse.

begin to weave in and out (C). The strands you *weave* under the first time will be woven *over* the next time, reversing with each row.

When one strand of yarn is finished, tie a new one onto

it with a tight knot, cutting ends close. Different colours can be woven in if desired.

When first disc is filled in, remove from loom by slipping loops off the notches. When the second circle is woven, turn them wrong side out, hold together and overcast or blanket-stitch together, leaving the top third free. This can be fastened with snaps, or the purse can be lined and a zip added.

For a handle, knot together six 14-inch strands of yarn. Make two more similar bundles, and braid these together ("Braiding", page 90). Knot on both ends and fasten across the side of the purse, or fasten on one side only, to dangle (D).

Woven Belt

To make a belt (Fig. 81), follow the pattern for the purse above. Make the loom 2 inches in diameter. Use yarn or

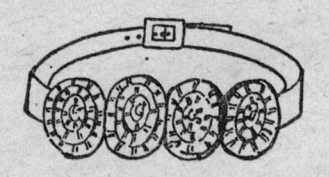

Fig. 81. Woven belt.

raffia, and make four discs. Stitch to a felt belt (see page 100). Buckle belt at back.

WHITTLING

Wood carving is a very old and very appealing hobby, and an easy one, say those who practise it. The main needs are soft wood (e.g. balsa), and a very sharp knife. No irresponsible person should take up this hobby. Whittling is for the careful.

WRITING

Writing a Story

It is sometimes hard to get started in writing a story. Often a picture in a magazine or book will seem to have a story behind it. Pick up a rock, or a penny, and write its tale. Observe a stranger closely, in a market or elsewhere, when he or she is not aware of it, and make up a story about him. Write a story or play with animals or toys as characters.

Picture Story

Write a story, but use a picture instead of a word whenever possible. Adjectives and nouns can be replaced with pictures, such as a tree for the word "tree". For "She was so happy", the word "happy" could be replaced with a tiny round face with a smile.

Writer's Motto

An old saying, given as advice by writers to those who wish to write, is this: "Attach the seat of the pants to the seat of the chair — and write." In other words, don't just *think* writing would be fun, but do it.

3
FUN WITH SCIENCE

Over twenty-five centuries ago men were beginning to realise that the physical world was governed by unchanging laws. Thus scientists of every type have been studying, experimenting with and observing these laws for a long time. Each generation's men of science have built on the knowledge written down for them by earlier students.

This chapter delves into eleven different fields of this vast store of knowledge.

HOW TO BE A SCIENTIST

1. Think your project through. Planning ahead saves time and money.

2. Read widely.

3. Question others. Talk with teachers, parents, other adults and school friends interested in the same field.

4. Work carefully as you go.

5. Do not be foolhardy. Dangerous materials should not be used by a young scientist except under supervision of an *informed* adult.

6. Observe carefully. Learn to *see* the world about you.

ASTRONOMY

Astronomy is the study of the heavens: the constellations, which are groups of stars that have seemed to form a pic-

Fun With Science

ture to all men everywhere since the dawn of history; the planets, which are satellites circling our most important star, the sun; and the stars themselves, the glowing heavenly bodies from which the planets reflect received light.

The planets and stars are not so difficult to learn if the memory tricks given in many books are mastered first.

The locations of the constellations at the four seasons may be found in a number of books, kits or charts. Such reference materials also show individual constellations with drawings picturing how they appeared to the Greeks who named them so long ago.

A moonless night is best for observation. With book or chart and flashlight locate the constellations. Then make "stargazers" (Fig. 83) so that you will know your favourite constellations without referring to a book.

Astronomy Experiments

To understand day and night, imagine a torch is the sun and a ball the earth. Darken the room and flash the torch on the ball. Turn the ball slowly from west (left) to east (right). This demonstrates how there can be dawn, daylight, twilight and night in different parts of the world at the same time.

TELESCOPE: Buy two lens holders and two inexpensive lenses: one thin convex lens, one thick convex lens.

Place lenses in lens holders. Turn a yard rule edge up, or

Fig. 82. Telescope.

piece of wood a yard long, and firmly wire the thin lens about one inch from one end of the stick. Wire the thick

lens one inch from the other end, but loosely enough to
move back and forth slightly (Fig. 82).

Use this telescope to make objects, including the moon,
seem larger and closer. Look from the thick-lens end,
adjusting this lens as necessary.

STARGAZERS: **1.** Save cardboard tubes from paper towels
toilet tissue, or foil. Stand a tube on black paper and cut a

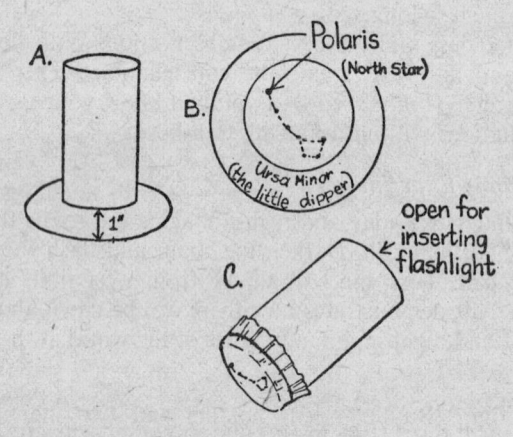

Fig. 83. Stargazer.

circle one inch larger all around, marking with a pencil the
rim of the tube on the larger circle (Fig. 83, A).

Within the tube mark, draw a constellation, following a
pattern from a book. Make a hole for each star using an
ordinary pin. Prick smaller holes for the dimmer stars (B).
Tie or tape the black circle to the end of the tube, or hold
with a rubber band (C). Label the name of the constellation
on the side. Use other tubes for other constellations. The
tubes may be painted if desired.

As a group activity, each person can make a different
constellation. When you know the constellations fairly well,
cover the names and see how many you can identify.

Fun With Science 115

The easiest way to observe through a "stargazer" is to go into a darkened room with torch. Flash the torch into the tube and aim it at the ceiling, where spots of light, shining through the pinpricks, will represent the constellation.

2. Use a cylindrical box. Remove the lid or one end. In the other punch out a diagram of a constellation. This will be more accurate if drawn on the box first to avoid errors in punching. Use as described under (1) above.

THE BODY

The study of the body is the science of physiology. Aristotle, who lived in Greece 2,500 years ago, discovered that the body has five basic senses — five completely different sensations. These are sight, sound, smell, taste and touch. Here are some experiments involving each:

Sight

OPTICAL ILLUSION: Cut from cardboard or white paper two 2-inch discs four 1-inch discs and four 3-inch discs. Glue these to two pieces of paper the same size, each paper centred by one of the 2-inch discs, combining one with the four 1-inch discs (Fig. 84, A) and the other with the 3-inch

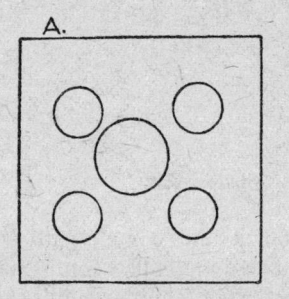

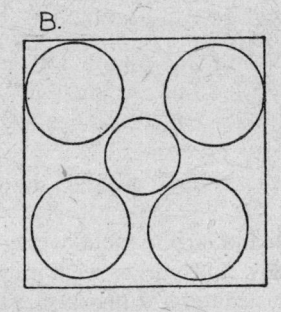

Fig. 84. Optical illusion discs.

discs (B). Hold the two papers a distance apart and ask someone which centre disc is larger. The disc in A will seem larger because the eye compares it to smaller surrounding discs. The disc in B will seem smaller.

COLOUR TRICKS: **1.** A rainbow is white light that has been bent at different angles by round drops of water in the atmosphere. To create a rainbow, get a thick, triangular piece of glass or a prism from a chandelier. Rotate it in the sun. These prisms bend the light just as does a rainbow, making ordinary white daylight change into rainbow colours.

2. Make a top as shown (Fig. 85, A) by cutting out discs of two colours such as blue and orange (B). Insert one into the other as shown in C and D, and spin. These will be some of the results you see: blue and orange seem white;

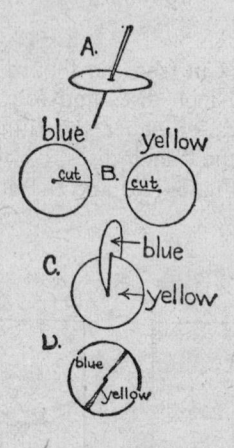

Fig. 85. Optical illusion top.

red and green seem white; black and white seem grey; yellow and purple seem grey. These are called complementary colours (opposites). Try experimenting with other combinations.

Fun With Science 117

Sound

A famous puzzle is this: If an oak tree fell in a field, and there was no one — animal or man — around to hear it, would there be sound? The answer is, surprisingly, there would be no sound, because sound is merely waves of air striking hearing apparatus. Sound waves travel much like the ripples on a quiet pond when a stone is dropped into the water, in ever widening circles.

Even if someone were there, he could *see* the tree fall almost simultaneously with its actual collapse, even if some distance away, because light travels at the speed of 186,000 miles per *second,* but if he were some distance away he would not *hear* the noise until several seconds later, because sound waves travel through air at approximately one-fifth of a mile (1,100 ft.) per second. Check this by watching a flash of lightning, and then listening for the delayed sound of its thunder. By counting the seconds slowly* and dividing by five you can estimate the number of miles it travelled.

A good test of hearing is to blindfold someone and strike two knives together to the right, to the left, in front and at the back, while he tries to identify the direction. If the subject's ears are normal, he will correctly locate the right and left sounds, but confuse the front and back, because the sound is striking both ears with the same intensity. This explains why it is not always easy to locate a distant aeroplane in the sky.

Taste

There are four basic tastes: sweet, salty, sour, bitter. These are reported to us by the senses. Foods such as meat and eggs are none of the basic four. We feel them with the tongue. The texture, taste and smell all combine to give us flavour.

The tongue has special taste buds. When we eat we use

---

* Most people count too rapidly to count by seconds. To time your count accurately, say "diddle diddle" between each number: "one- diddle diddle — two- diddle diddle — three . . .", etc.

the full tongue, but a lollipop can be enjoyed more by *licking* because the sweet taste buds are at the tip of the tongue. A pill tastes bitter after it goes down because the bitter taste buds are at the back of the tongue.

EXPERIMENTS: Into a small bottle or glass squeeze some lemon juice and fill with water. Use the same amount of tonic water for a type of somewhat bitter sample, ¼ teaspoon sugar to water for the sweet, and a few dashes of salt to water for the salty. Use four medicine droppers or one washed well after each experiment.

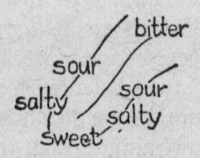

Fig. 86. Taste areas of the tongue.

Drop one or two drops of sugar water on the tip of the tongue, and shortly after repeat on the back of the tongue. The taste will be less sweet there and disappear sooner.

Repeat with each sample, following the chart of the tongue shown (Fig. 86). You will find that tonic, for example, has a very different taste on the front of the tongue from its taste on the back. Try a very small taste of Epsom salts on the back and then on the front of the tongue. Its taste, too, you will find, depends upon its placement.

(See also "Food experiments" later in this chapter.)

Touch

1. Have someone sit down, close his eyes and bend slightly forward. With two toothpicks touch him on the back of the neck, sometimes far apart, sometimes with just one. Have him indicate whether he is being touched with one or two, and where. Now try the toothpicks on the fingers, with the person still blindfolded. You will discover that the subject can identify finger touch much more accurately.

Fingers have many more nerve endings than the back of the neck, because one of the purposes of the hands is to touch and identify. This experiment explains why a very tiny cut on the tip of the finger may hurt more and longer than a large, deeper scratch on the leg, for example.

2. Whenever you accidentally tear a piece of skin that must be cut away, look at it under the microscope if possible. You will see an outer scale-like layer, the epidermis, which is dead and is being constantly sloughed off. This protects the dermis, or live skin, which can be seen underneath. The outer skin has no nerve endings. To prove this, think back :

Nearly everyone has at some time run a pin or needle through a very small, shallow area of skin. Or you may have very lightly stabbed yourself with a pin, so that the point barely pricked the surface, but hung there. You will recall that neither experience hurt. On the other hand, almost everyone can remember the pain of a graze on knee or elbow, received while falling in the playground. The difference in degree of pain is due to the fact that the pins pricked only the epidermis, where there are no nerves, hence no feeling. The falls scraped off the protective epidermis, leaving the dermis, with its nerve endings exposed.

3. To discover why office managers insist that thermostats (set at say 68°) or thermometers instead of feelings should be used to regulate the heat of a room, try these experiments :

Place a hand in a bowl of water as hot as endurable. At first it will be necessary to remove your hand once or twice. However, before the water has had time to cool greatly, the hand will be able to endure it for quite a long period. It has become accustomed to the heat, just as someone in an over-heated room becomes accustomed to it.

When the hand has had time to return to its normal temperature, prepare three bowls of water: one very warm, one very cold, one lukewarm. Keep the left hand in the cold water, the right hand in the hot water, for a time.

Then place both hands in the tepid water. It will feel warm to the hand from the cold water, cold to the hand from the hot water.

These experiments will explain why, when you enter a house from the outside in winter, it may feel very warm when it is not. When coming from an overheated kitchen, the lounge may feel too cool when in reality it is not. The temptation to adjust the heat will pass as the body adjusts. But a thermostat or thermometer cannot be fooled.

CHEMISTRY

The entire world is made up of 92 naturally occurring physical substances (elements), plus more created in nuclear reactors by the breakdown of atoms. Chemistry is the study of these elements and how they react when combined with or separated from each other. Of the thousands of experiments awaiting the young scientist who wishes to explore the science of chemistry, here are two:

Heat

Some materials are excellent conductors of heat. Some are poor conductors. Each has a job to do. Experiment: Hold a match against low heat on the stove. The wood of the match will remain cool even when the match ignites and burns almost to the fingers, because wood is a poor conductor of heat. Now place an empty pan on that low heat briefly and hold a hand flat against the bottom for a moment. The metal pan, an excellent conductor, gets hot almost immediately. This is one of the reasons why cooking utensils are not made of wood — it burns before it conducts heat — but their handles may be. This experiment indicates the reason for many of the common uses of wood and metal.

To discover which would make better camp drinking cups, plastic or aluminium, pour hot water into both a plastic cup and a metal measuring cup. The hot drink will immediately heat the aluminium cup, making it too hot for lip and hand. Because the cup conducts the heat *from* the liquid, the drink also cools too quickly.

Absorption

Plants draw water and food up through their trunks and stems to sustain life. To prove this, place white flowers or blossom in water coloured with food colouring.

Paper manufacturing companies use this same principle of *absorption* in deciding what type of paper to create for specific purposes. To test this, place a piece of waxed paper and a strip of paper towel or newspaper in a bowl of water. The wax coating on the one prevents water from soaking in, but paper towels are made to aborb water, and newsprint is absorbent to keep ink from smearing. Each type of paper in the house possesses its special qualities because of the job it must do, as testing will show. Test paper drinking cups, face tissues, writing paper, blotting paper.

CRIME DETECTION

The brave men who served as "peelers" or policemen of Victorian London would marvel at the tools that science, mostly chemistry, has given to the police at Scotland Yard today.

One of the most important tools is fingerprinting. Fingerprints are the result of the natural oils of the skin clinging to the surface of objects handled. The prints of no two fingers are alike; thus a careless criminal leaves a calling card when he leaves a fingerprint — a difficult thing to prevent, because wearing gloves makes the fingers clumsy.

To study this procedure, make a fingerprint powder by mixing $\frac{1}{4}$ cup of baking powder with $\frac{1}{4}$ cup of carbon (lampblack). Handle a dish or saucer, then sprinkle some fingerprint powder over the area, brushing very gently with a stretched-out piece of thin cotton. Gently knock off excess powder to reveal the fingerprint.

Another tool is the microscope. Carefully lay a strip of sellotape over the powdered fingerprint, transferring the print to the tape. Stick this to a glass microscope slide and study it. If no microscope is available use a magnifying glass, still another excellent tool. Make fingerprints of several people and compare.

For footprints, step in soft earth, then make a plaster cast (see page 17).

Photographs of the scene of the crime are another constantly used crime tool. (To study photography, see "Photography", page 98.)

FOODS

The study of foods is the science of nutrition. Scientists have discovered that man needs seven basic foods daily: (1) butter or fortified margarine; (2) citrus fruits; (3) at least two green vegetables — a green salad would count as one vegetable; (4) yellow vegetable or potatoes; (5) eggs, *wholegrain* wheat, or meat (bacon does not count); (6) one other fruit; (7) milk.

Experiments

1. Check your own diet for a full day, to see if it has included something from each group.

2. The basic foods above give us the tools of life: proteins, minerals, vitamins, fats and carbohydrates. Almost everyone in Britain gets enough, and often too much, of the last two. The first three tools, proteins, vitamins and minerals, are easily destroyed or discarded if improperly handled. Nature often steers us away from unsuitable foods by making them taste less appetising when they have lost their vital elements. Test this by these methods:

Eat some green peas, raw, the day they are purchased. Leave a pod or two of the fresh peas in the refrigerator for a week, then taste. Leave a pod, plus a few peas out of another pod, on the kitchen table for a few days; and taste.

The results will be surprising. If the peas were fresh and

refrigerated at the shop, the pods will be crisp and the peas sweet when eaten raw the first day. The peas left exposed on the table for a few days will wither and lose both juice and taste. The pod on the table will wither and the peas will lose flavour, as the sugar turns to starch. Even refrigerated peas kept for a week will lose some flavour — and some food value.

This experiment will produce the same results with sweet corn, carrots, parsley, peeled potatoes and other fresh foods. In a week it will become evident that potatoes should not be peeled until used, carrots should be refrigerated and kept crisp in a plastic bag, parsley in a covered jar or plastic bag. Sweet corn should be frozen or used in a day or two to prevent the sugar changing to starch. When foods are crisp and sweet they also contain more body builders.

3. Open an orange. Eat half immediately, leave half exposed on the table for a day or night and then eat. The very taste of the exposed orange will indicate loss of both flavour and Vitamin C.

GEOGRAPHY

This is the study of the earth's surface — the "lay of the land". Use a long potato cut in half lengthwise to make a chart, showing the altitude of various areas (their distances above sea level).

To do this, find a topographical map in a map book or

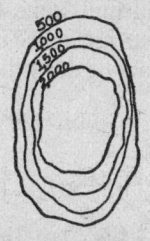

Fig. 87. Altitude lines of a map, made with a potato.

encyclopedia. It will contain circles showing the different altitudes. These are often in different colours. Now choose one small area to chart. This is especially interesting with a map of one's own area and you can use a small-scale Ordnance Survey map.

The full half of the potato is laid, open side down, on a sheet of paper, and the outline drawn. Remove potato and cut away a ¼-inch slice from the open side. Now lay the reduced-in-size potato in the middle of its former outline and draw its present outline (Fig. 87). Cut off as many slices as there are altitudes given in the section being charted and draw one within the other. Label with the proper distances above sea level, as shown, or colour, making a key in the corner (red for 1,000 feet, yellow for 2,000, and so on). After each tiny square of colour in the key, write the altitude it represents.

GEOLOGY

This is the study of how the earth beneath our feet came to be. Here is just one experiment as a starter :

When travelling or picnicking, find a cutting that exposes layers (strata) of rock, or locate an exposed rocky cliff. Study the strata. They will show how the earth is pushed and buckled to make mountains. You may be fortunate and find the fossil (rock outline) of an ancient plant or animal, even a seashell, proving that some inland area was once covered with water.

With a sharp stick or penknife try to chip away the various strata. You will find some layers that chip easily, others that are not even nicked. This will show you why rain and wind erode (carry away) the land unevenly, forming hills and gullies.

PERSPECTIVE

Perspective is one of the science tools of art. It is the

relation between the size of an object and its distance from the eye. To understand this, go to the back door and look outside. The closest trees or buildings seem to be much taller than the trees or buildings farther away, even when they actually are the same size.

Experiments

1. Draw a railway line or an avenue of trees on a sheet of paper. Begin at the centre bottom and draw the lines or trees straight to the top of the page. To check accuracy, see Fig. 88, which demonstrates the way the eye actually sees

Fig. 88. A parallel line of trees as they appear to the eye.

two parallel lines in the distance. The lines seem to come together because the eye is no longer able to distinguish the space between them. In drawing, such lines are not actually shown parallel, but come together at the top (the horizon) to form a long triangle, and the objects grow smaller. The next time you see a railway line or avenue, observe them closely for perspective.

2. Sketch your back yard. Be sure to note the size of a

dog, birds, fences, trees or buildings when seen close to you or to each other, as compared with those farther away.

PHYSICS

This is the study of the unchanging laws that govern the universe. Discoveries in this one field of science have brought more changes in our knowledge in recent years than have discoveries in any other field. Consider the almost unbelievable discovery that electromagnetic impulses travel through the vacuum of space from the stars, resulting in radio, radar, TV, light, even X-rays.* Consider man-made moons and shooting rockets into space, something out of *Star Trek* — or so it seemed until very recent years.

Experiments

1. Here is the scientific law that makes possible the development of jets and missiles: *For every action there is a reaction.* Make a rocket to prove this.

Cut a light-weight piece of cardboard one inch square. Punch a hole in the centre and push a pencil through. Through this hole pull the mouth of a long balloon; blow up until solid. Hold closed and point upward. Gradually open fingers. As air begins to release, let go. The air pushing *back* (action) forces the balloon *forward* (reaction). This explains why rockets and jets have streaming tails.

2. To understand why satellites remain in space so long, consider another scientific fact, the law of inertia: *Objects at rest tend to remain at rest; objects in movement tend to remain in movement.* To test this, run an 18-inch string through a cotton reel. To one end tie a small ball, enclosed in old curtain material or other light fabric. To the other end of the string tie a small rock or fairly heavy bolt. Hold the bolt in one hand, the cotton reel in the other, and whirl

---

* The author is indebted to Neill Ostrander, physicist of Systems Laboratories, Sherman Oaks, California, for assistance with the sections on "Physics" and "Chemistry".

Fun With Science　　　　　　　　　　　　　　　　　　　　　127

the ball over the head. When the ball is whirling fast enough, you can release the weight, which will climb to the reel.

As long as the *speed* of the ball is balanced by the *weight* of the bolt, the ball (satellite) remains in position, because the *centripetal* force of the weight (gravity, pulling it down), is balanced by *centrifugal* force of the ball (its inertia, causing it to keep going by flying out). When the ball whirls fast enough, its speed overbalances the bolt, pulling it up. If the whirling slows, the ball drops nearer the spool as gravity overbalances inertia. Cut the string while the ball is whirling rapidly. It will fly outward, for there is no force of gravity to balance the inertia, until its speed fails and gravity pulls it down.

Scientists have studied the speed necessary for the space satellites to balance the force of gravity *just enough* to remain "in orbit", going around the earth.

Watch lorries and cars stopping and starting at traffic lights to see how inertia affects all still or moving objects. Lorries, because of greater weight, both stop and start more slowly. Note, however, that even cars take considerable space and time to stop, an important fact for cyclists and pedestrians to remember.

SOIL CONSERVATION

Soil is the pulverised rock and debris of the centuries. The topsoil is the most valuable — and the most likely to be washed away. Men until recently did not understand this or know how to prevent it, and thus a great deal of fertile land was destroyed.

To see how this happens, get two cartons of the same size from the supermarket. Cut the two sides and an end of each to three inches deep, the other end to one inch deep (Fig. 8). Fill with about two inches of soil, packed down somewhat tightly, but moulded like a hill on the shallow end, as shown (A).

On the higher end of one box (B) dig a furrow with your finger across the end and parallel to it. From this extend long furrows running straight down to the shallow end. In the other box (C) connect the same type of top furrow with another parallel to it, going across the box, and so on down

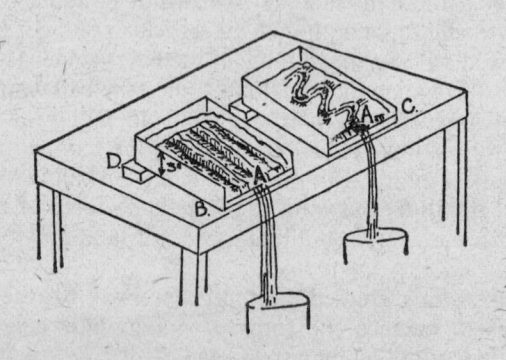

Fig. 89. Soil conservation study.

to the shallow end, like a long unbroken coil, back and forth until the last parallel row curves gently to the edge.

Set each box where draining mud can be observed but will cause no damage, and tilt slightly with the deep end raised (D).

The miniature ploughed fields are now ready for rain. Trickle a small stream of water into the higher end of each box, and compare. Either use two hoses simultaneously or time the trickling, and see which box shows more moisture by the end of perhaps three minutes. (You can also tell which holds more moisture by lifting. The soil that retains the water will be heavier.) The box with the coiled furrows (C), similar to modern contour ploughing, will prove the better type in all ways: the water takes longer to pass through, causing more of it to sink in, instead of draining off, and the same box will lose less topsoil.

WEATHER

Many people or organisations such as farmers and air-

Fun With Science

lines need dependable weather predictions. Weathermen (meteorologists) are hoping to discover new facts about the atmosphere from our man-made satellites, in order to improve their ability to predict weather. To understand their need, try this experiment:

On a large sheet of paper, make a calendar for the current month, or use a spare one that possesses big spaces. Make the lines with coloured crayon, and divide each day's square in half horizontally as in Fig. 90 with pencilled lines.

Each night read the newspaper's weather prediction for the coming day or watch the forecast on television. If sun-

Fig. 90. Calendar for checking on the weatherman.

shine is predicted, draw a little sun in the *upper* half of tomorrow's square. If rain is predicted, draw raindrops or an umbrella; if cloudy, draw a cloud. Thus the upper half of each day is the prediction. At the end of each day, draw in the *lower* half the symbol that most nearly indicates what the weather actually was.

At the end of the month make a key in the corner. Draw each symbol used and opposite it give the number of days of each kind of weather. Below list the number of times the weatherman was wrong.

Rain Gauge

After a heavy rain there are often several inches of water in a pan left outdoors, and yet the official record may list only half an inch of rainfall for the area. This is because weather stations have a gauge that measures rainfall by the amount of rain that falls in one cubic inch of space.

To make a fairly accurate home gauge, get a one-inch beaker, a special type of glass jar, from a chemist, school supply or hobby shop. If it is not marked, very carefully label it with inches and quarter inches, using fine lines of

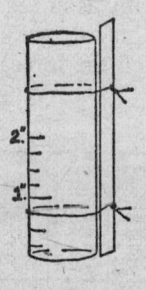

Fig. 91. Rain gauge.

nail varnish (Fig. 91). Wire the beaker to a board, leaving the holding wire loose enough to remove for emptying. Nail or wire the board to a fence post or other spot that is exposed to the sky from all sides. Check and empty after each storm.

4
NATURE LORE

*So live that in a future year,
None will regret that you passed here.**

This should be the motto of the true nature lover. If you can picnic or camp or hike in the beautiful outdoors of Great Britain and *leave no record*, you will be welcome everywhere — and welcomed back. If you leave a trail of destroyed plants, paper or tin cans, then others truly *will* regret that you "passed here".

NATURE HOBBIES

Here are many special fields of interest for those who enjoy the outdoors, and ways of saving its treasures.

ANIMALS

Make a collection of small animals from nature objects: cones, nuts, shells, acorns, feathers. For ideas, using cotton, yarn and other materials, see "Animals", page 18. See also "Pets", page 98 and "Wild Pets", this chapter.

---

* Adapted from a poem by Woodbridge Metcalf of the California Conservation Council.

AQUARIUM

An aquarium is a balanced water-world, wherein the fish and snails take in oxygen and breathe out carbon dioxide, while the plants do the opposite.

To keep fish, such as the miniature goldfish that are the least expensive and easiest to raise, buy plant greenery for them where the fish are obtained. Add a small pinch of commercial food daily. Clean the bowl once a week by scooping out the fish with hands or dip net (see Fig. 92) and placing them in a jar of water that has set for an hour or two — water must be room temperature. Scrub the bowl, fill with tap water and again let set. Add shells for interest, replace the greenery when eaten, and pour the fish back. Add water when it evaporates, and keep the aquarium out of the sunlight.

In a true aquarium, the plants are actually planted in an inch of sand or gravel that has been thoroughly washed free of dirt first. Lay paper over the plants to prevent uprooting, and carefully pour in water. Remove paper, wait until water is room temperature and add tadpoles, snails or fish.

BIRDS

Bird watchers see many amusing and amazing sights. A kingfisher dashes colourfully in and out of the trees above the river. A sparrow does a queer dance; he is hopping forward, scratching back — uncovering the new grass seed just planted. Sharp observation will reveal a fascinating world.

Here are a few rules for bird watching: (1) Remain quiet. (2) Move slowly. (3) Keep a distance; don't look in nests unless sure they are abandoned. (4) Don't collect nests or eggs unless abandoned. (5) Make notes on the spot, to prevent forgetting or getting confused.

Points to record when possible: (1) Where the bird was seen (in a pine tree, in a meadow, etc.). (2) What it was eating. (3) How large it is, what colour, what kind of bill, how it flies. (4) What is its call? (5) Was it alone or with many others? (6) Type of nest and eggs (climbing to observe may drive a mother bird away never to return, but ground nests present less of a problem).

Make a list of the points above, then look up the bird in a book or chart. Take books when travelling. Keep a neat, permanent notebook with your own information and notes, plus the name and page number of the book where information and pictures were found.

Birds' Nests

It is possible in late autumn or winter to find nests deserted by their small builders and easily seen in the bare branches. Cut out branch and all when small and not important to the tree, or remove nest with care, to prevent destruction.

Occasionally abandoned eggs can be found to fill the nests. You may discover (without observing too closely) that a long-watched back-yard nest has been deserted by the mother bird. Or eggs or parts of shells are sometimes found on the ground beneath a nest.

Since finding eggs that may be taken is a rare thing, making clay or plaster eggs of the proper size and painting them adds interest to the collection. See bird books for examples.

Experiments

1. Carefully pull a bird's nest apart and list the materials it contains. Study the weaving of the nest — some birds make much finer nests than others. If you already know what bird built the nest, write a description of it for your scrapbook, with other material on the same bird.

2. Plant a bird's nest in a flower pot, covering with $\frac{1}{2}$ inch of soil.

Keep moist, and when it sprouts, try to identify what comes up. This reveals the needs for that type of bird, both for nesting materials and food. This information also should go into the bird notebook.

FLOWERS

The best rule for wild flowers is to leave them as nature intended. They are becoming all too rare and fade before they can be brought home for a bouquet. For a pressed-flower scrapbook, pick them only where they are in abundance, and press immediately.

To press, place a section of newspaper on a hard surface, then wax paper, the flower, more wax paper, and finally several heavy books. When thoroughly dry, tape to a scrapbook page. When sketching, draw in the natural background: moorland, woodland, field. In the corner of page give name, if possible, and where found.

INSECTS

Two methods of collecting insects may be followed. The more difficult is to have sets showing the life cycle of individual insects. The second method is to collect adult insects, such as butterflies.

The easiest method of following a life cycle is to raise insects. In winter or early spring, look for cocoons, gently detach (with a section of twig if possible) and place in a half-gallon jar with a wide mouth, obtained from restaurants. Punch several air holes in the lid.

One day an adult insect will emerge. If it is a female, it will lay eggs in the jar. Watch for this. Egg-laying occurs within several hours after she emerges from the chrysalis.

When caterpillars emerge from the eggs, around two weeks, begin to drop a few leaves into the jar. Experiment to find the types preferred. Begin with those of plants closest to the place where the cocoon was obtained.

Constant feeding should produce at least a few caterpillars which survive all the skin changes and other hazards, to change, in about two months, back into the pupa stage, which also lasts around two months, thus completing the life cycle.

Nature Lore 135

Butterfly Net

To catch butterflies and moths, find a bamboo pole (best because it is light), or other long stick such as a broom handle. Bend a wire clothes hanger into a circle, and straighten the curved hanger-top. Cut a piece of muslin or old net curtains 38 by 40 inches. Across the top (at 38-inch

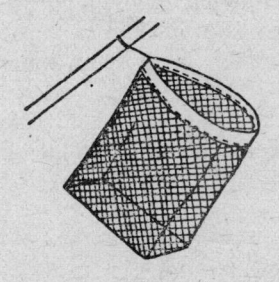

Fig. 92. Butterfly net. In miniature this can be a dip net.

end) stitch a border of wide mending tape. Double the material and stitch down the side. Stitch the bottom hem to a 12-inch square of similar material. Sew the taped top over the wire loop, attach the straightened top of the hanger to the pole with wire, and the butterfly net is complete (Fig. 92).

ROCKS

Rock and Stone Collection

A rock collection can be just a group of rocks and stones, but it is more interesting to read about the rocks in books and learn to identify the collection by type. Rocks can be grouped by their natural location (North Downs flints), or by their type (igneous, sedimentary, metamorphic).

Try to keep the specimens as near the same size as possible to add uniformity to the collection. Mount on heavy corrugated paper cut from cartons and painted, or in plaster of Paris casts, or in boxes, by gluing. Before gluing, use a fine brush or toothpick to paint a number on the rock in India ink, white enamel or nail varnish. On a label below the mounting, or in the lid of the box, or on a separate chart, opposite that same number list these facts when possible: the name of the rock, the type, where and when found, and uses.

Rocks can be collected also to illustrate the geology of the world. One rock might expose a particularly interesting bit of strata (layers showing the passage of time just as tree rings do). Another might show water erosion, or an embedded fossil.

Look for a lapidary shop in your area where stones may be seen and identified. This will help identify the specimens in your collection.

THE SEA AND SHELLS

Skin diving and glass-bottom boats may not be within everyone's reach, but many films have been made showing the wonders of the sea. Watch for these. Keep a scrapbook. Make drawings of seaweed and collections of shells (below). Become a beachcomber, looking for interesting deadwood, glass fragments and other objects washed up by the sea.

Shell Collection

The best time to collect shells is when the tide is far out, or in the early morning before the beach has been picked clean of unusual varieties.

Shells can be mounted with household glue on heavy corrugated paper cut from a carton and painted or covered. They can be mounted on a thin board, or "free" form such as a flat piece of driftwood. Small shells can be kept in moulded egg cartons. They can be grouped by related families, such as varieties of limpets, or by locations where found, such as Cornwall or Guernsey.

Write or paste in, below each shell, its name when possible, and where and when found. (To mount in plaster of Paris, see page 15.)

TREES

If trees are taken for a hobby, a scrapbook of pictures or drawings can be made, or separate collections, such as woods, leaves, twigs, seeds, can be made. Or each tree may be taken individually with everything pertaining to it displayed on one card.

Make cards of equal size from supermarket cartons; around 8 to 10 inches is a satisfactory size. Sketch a picture of the tree in one corner, or cut one from a book and paste down. Sketch the blossom if possible. Then, to the same piece of cardboard, glue a sample of wood, a twig, a leaf, seeds and seed pods, cones, etc. Label with the name of the tree, tell where found, give uses.

To study trees, learn to recognise different types by the following: leaves, twigs, way of branching, size, place of growth, fruits, blossoms, berries, nuts or cones, bark.

Learn the uses of trees: for man, as food, fuel, building material, paper, or other products; for animals, as food or shelter; and for plants, as shelter or soil conditioner. Make sketches of leaves, tree products, and the trees themselves, for the tree scrapbook.

See "Nature Crafts" later in this section for things to do with leaves, bark, etc.

Leaf Collection

Leaves should be pressed to make a good collection. Place leaves on five or six sheets of newspaper on a board or other flat surface, cover with newspaper, top with another flat surface and weight heavily with books or rocks.

When thoroughly dry, tape or glue the leaves to a scrapbook page or piece of cardboard. Paste a label beneath, or write in the name of the tree, where found, its type and uses. If possible, sketch a picture of the tree. To glue to smooth or slippery surfaces such as oil cloth or glass, use a mixture of glue and vinegar in equal parts, pressing until dry.

LEAF PRINTS: These may be made in a number of ways.

1. **Wax mounting:** Press fresh-picked coloured leaves

between two sheets of heavy wax paper, using a warm iron, then mount in a scrapbook with tape or glue.

2. Crayon print: Place a section of newspaper or a magazine on a work area to give a soft surface. Lay the leaf on this with the underside (vein side) up. Over this place thin drawing paper, hold carefully, and colour the leaf area solidly with the side or flat end of a soft crayon, choosing green or other autumn leaf colours. Make all strokes go in the same direction. Cut out along the leaf outline and mount in a scrapbook.

3. Ink print: Cut a piece of felt the size of the largest leaf on hand. Place felt on a board or glass and carefully pour on some ink until well-moistened. Place leaf on this, vein-side down, cover with heavy paper and run a hand or roller over it carefully. Then lift the leaf, being *very* careful not to smear, place it on plain paper, and again roll or press. Be sure to permit thorough drying. If ink printing is well done, it is the best type for a scrapbook because it shows veining so clearly. Tubes of printer's ink from a stationery shop are best for this, but not necessary. Green is the best colour.

4. Clay print: For this, use a perfect, wide, attractive leaf such as sycamore. Use a permanent type of clay that needs no kiln-drying for a lasting print. Roll out a piece of clay ¼-inch thick and at least as large as the leaf to be cast. Lay the leaf on the clay, vein-side down, and roll carefully with rolling pin, then cut out the outline of the leaf with a knife or a paper clip opened out. Carefully curl the edges of the clay to resemble real leaf, and then place rolls of clay under the curled edges to hold in position while drying. Cover with a damp cloth to permit even drying. When thoroughly dry (several days later), paint with art enamel from a stationery shop. This makes an attractive ash tray or dish.

Seed Collection

A seed collection can include not only the seeds but their

protectors: cones, pods, thistles, "parachutes", and "wings".

Place the seeds themselves in the centre of a small piece of transparent plastic paper. Fold up to form an envelope, seal the three open sides with tape and attach the top with tape to a cardboard, with a label to identify the seed and tell where found. On this same card glue the seed protector. If the tree or plant has been observed through the seasons, sketch pictures of the stages of development. With a cherry seed, for example, show the spring blossom and summer fruit from which the seed came.

Twig Identification

Identifying twigs of deciduous trees (those that lose their leaves in winter) takes care and study. The best time to collect is in late winter or early spring. Label each twig when collected, to prevent mixing them. Cut off two 6-inch tips, cutting at a sharp angle to expose the interior better.

Tie or sellotape one twig of each type of tree to the twig collection cardboard, or to the tree collection. Place the other twig in deep water. If possible, sketch the buds and leaves as the twig in water begins to open, and place this with the twig from the same tree. A few comparisons will quickly show how even "dead" branches differ.

Wood collections: When dead branches are available, choose bark-covered samples of various woods that are perhaps one inch around, 5 inches long. Cut the sample half way down through the centre and slice off as shown (Fig.

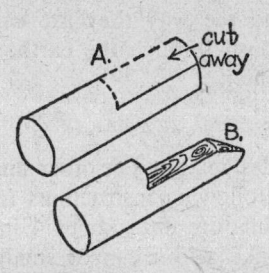

Fig. 93. Wood cut to show the grain.

93, A) to display the grain. On the sliced end make a slanting cut as shown (B), to show the quarter grain. Sandpaper and varnish the cut surfaces.

Drawing pin a card to the piece of wood, stating type, uses, where found. Or glue the wood into a box with card pasted beneath.

With live wood, the cutting must be seasoned by permitting it to dry thoroughly, before adapting it to a collection.

WILD PETS

It is difficult to keep wild pets, which seldom eat well in captivity. It is better to observe them a few days and then release them.

For information on grasshoppers, ants, spiders and many other small creatures as pets, see an encyclopedia.

Earthworms

Use a pint jar with a wide mouth and a lid punched with holes. When not observing, place the jar in a brown paper bag and fasten the bag with a rubber band to the rim of the jar. Spread the bag open above the rubber band and cut the top off about two inches above the lid.

Nearly fill the jar with moist, loosely packed earth and perhaps four earthworms. For food place bits of bread dipped in milk, leftover porridge or mashed potatoes at the top. Change the food daily.

To observe, take the jar from the bag. Watch the growth of the worms and see why they are called the farmer's friends, as they push through the earth, "ploughing" and permitting air to enter.

Tadpoles

To catch tadpoles, minnows or other small water animals, make a dip net, following instructions for a butterfly net (Fig. 92) in a miniature size, about 4 inches around and 5 inches deep. Take also a can or small bucket, because they should be kept in the water in which they were found.

Nature Lore

To make a handle for the can, punch holes opposite each other near the rim and tie a string handle.

Bring home scum, sticks and plants with the animals. Place in a large jar or aquarium. When the tadpoles become frogs they need a stone or stick protruding from the water, or a cork, to rest on, and bits of lettuce for food.

When they turn into frogs free them or place in a terrarium (see page 144). They need flies, insects and meat bits to eat, but since they catch moving food, it should be suspended on tweezers or thread and moved.

NATURE CRAFTS

Diorama

A diorama is a scene built into a box. Use a small wooden box, or sturdy cardboard boxes of small size, or half-gallon ice cream containers. Cut one side and the top away. With the ice cream container, cut away a third of the side but none of the bottom.

For the floor surface use real moss or lichen, sand, plaster of Paris, papier mâché, or clay or real grass. Bits of sponge,

Fig. 94. Diorama.

especially if coloured already or dried with coloured poster paint in them, serve as bushes. Use foil as water; place blue or green paper beneath, and place clay, grass or other substance over the edge to give natural, uneven borders. Use stones and pebbles for boulders. Rather thick twigs can serve as logs or bridges. Animals, fences, human figures, boats, cars, and so on, all can be toy miniatures or pipe-cleaner figures (see page 70). The surface can be painted to resemble grass sprayed with Christmas snow. The walls of the carton can be painted to resemble a blue sky, perhaps with scudding clouds, painted white or made of thin cotton (Fig. 94).

Shadow Boxes

CIGAR BOX: This is a variety of textured painting (see page 26).

Ask a tobacconist to save a flat, one-inch-deep cigar box. Tear off the paper or cover with a damp cloth *just* long enough to remove paper. When dry, sand lightly if necessary. Paint the outside a colour to harmonise with the room in which it will hang. Paint the inside blue (for sky).

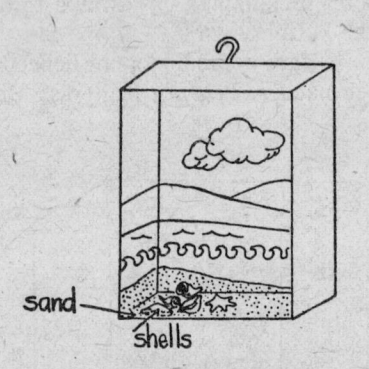

Fig. 95. Cigar box shadow box.

Draw a design on paper first, to prevent errors. Plan the scene to suit miniature nature objects that are easily collected. For example, moss or lichen (from woods or hobby shop), small twigs, some pebbles, sand, can provide materials for a picture of a tree (twig for a trunk, lichen for leaves), a stream with real sand sprinkled on glue at the edge, with the pebbles as rocks (see Fig. 95). A bridge can be made of twigs, flowers of crêpe paper. Miniature shells can be used for a shore scene. Each item is glued to floor or back. Objects needed for the scene may be made from papier mâché or crêpe or craft paper.

SARDINE-CAN SHADOW BOX: Use a sardine can of any type. This can be painted first if desired, for added colour. Glue a piece of blue craft paper to the inside bottom, or paint blue, for background. To this background, glue tiny sprigs of dried grains or grasses, seed pods, etc., in a pleasing arrangement (Fig. 96).

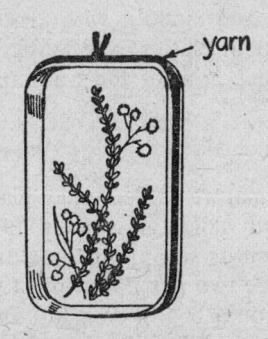

Fig. 96. Sardine can shadow box.

Run a piece of carpet thread or braided wool around the outside rim and tie at the top, with a loop to hang the box. If desired, a small piece of cling film can be placed over the box as "glass". The yarn can be tied over this to hold it.

Small shadow boxes are even more attractive if hung in pairs or fours with different arrangements in each.

Woodland Tracks

To keep a permanent record of the animal tracks that are so exciting to find, take supplies for making plaster casts when travelling. A shoebox or ice cream carton will hold cardboard and paper clips, or low cans such as tuna and salmon come in, for frames; also: plaster of Paris powder, a tin can, Vaseline, and talcum. Carry a container of water.

When a track is found, cut a one-inch strip of cardboard long enough to circle the track, clip ends together with a paperclip, and press gently into the earth, to hold the mould. Or cut both ends from a low can large enough to circle the track and press it into the ground. Lightly sprinkle the track with talcum.

Use a tin can to mix plaster of Paris with water to the consistency of cream; add a pinch of salt if in a hurry, and carefully pour over the track. This will harden in ten minutes. Then the mould can be removed and the cast cleaned. It is now like a negative of a photograph — just backward. To make a positive cast, coat the negative cast with Vaseline and circle it with a new cardboard or can frame. Again pour plaster over it. When this hardens, there will be an exact print of the track to add to your home museum.

Terrarium

This is a miniature garden under glass. Use an aquarium or a wide-mouth gallon glass jar from a restaurant. If a jar is used, lay it on its side and make a frame to prevent rolling. This can be two narrow strips of wood nailed parallel to each other on a board, with just enough room between them to rest the jar. Paint the base for neatness.

A terrarium can be made of woodland or bog plants, or cultivated ones. It should be arranged as a scene. First bits of gravel or broken flower pots are scattered, then sand into which charcoal is pressed. Over this sprinkle one or two inches of the type of soil the particular plants require. This can be built into "hills" for interest. Rocks can be added for boulders, a small glass dish with pebbles in it for a pool.

The plants should be placed far enough apart to avoid crowding. Native insects or animals (lizards, baby frogs) may be added. Water preferably with a fine spray. Since a terrarium has a lid, usually one that permits little air to enter, however, watering is needed very infrequently, possibly only once a month. When a slight mist clings to the glass the terrarium has enough water.

Nature Jewellery

String nature items together on a wire or heavy cord, long enough to permit the hand to squeeze through, for a bracelet, or to go over the head for a necklace. Use acorn cups, small nuts or acorns, tough seed pods, shells. Follow a pattern, such as placing two acorn cups back to back, followed by a small acorn, and repeating.

Map Making

Sketch a map of an area while looking down on it from a hill, or map a footpath or your home area while walking.

Be consistent in the use of symbols, using the same symbol for the same feature each time, such as two lines running closely parallel for streams, one line for roads, etc. Proportions should be as accurate as possible. In a lower corner, make a "legend", showing the sign used for each feature.

Reed Basket

Soak reeds (found in marsh or hobby shop) in water for one half hour, then lay four one-foot reeds on a table. Lay

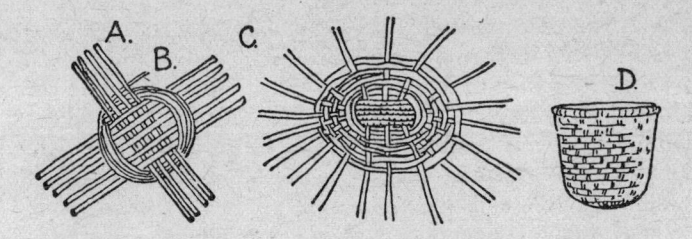

Fig. 97. Reed basketmaking.

five one-foot reeds on top in the other direction, as shown (Fig. 97, A). Run a long reed around these "warp" reeds, under all four, over all five (B), pressing close together as you work. Begin a second reed where the first ends. On the fifth full round, spread the reeds in a sunburst as you weave, going over one reed, under the next (C). Reeds and basket should be dipped in water frequently as the work progresses, to prevent breaking. See finished basket (D). Glue down the last two inches of the top row to prevent unravelling.

Ink Prints

See page 138 for method. In addition to leaves, fern fronds and flowers can be ink-printed, preferably after pressing for an hour or two. If printer's ink is used, clean the glass with turpentine when finished. Printer's ink is not washable, so protect clothes.

Toys to Make

Use cones, seeds, nuts, acorns, pods, twigs, feathers, for materials. Create animals, men, birds, trees, plants. Hold together with picture wire, pipe cleaners, or glue. This is an excellent party craft.

Plaster of Paris Casts and Mounts

Casts may be made of animal tracks, leaves, ferns, flowers, twigs, seeds, rocks or shells. For collections, if it is desired to mount more than one specimen on one cast, all specimens must be on hand when the mould is made, for plaster hardens fast and cannot be remoulded.

To make casts, roll out on paper some Plasticine (soft clay) the size of the mould wanted and about ½-inch thick. Roll smooth and press or roll the specimens into the clay deeply enough to show veins, fern spore cases and the like. Remove the specimens and cut a piece of cardboard two inches wide and long enough to fit around the edge of the clay. Join ends with paper clips. Pour in the plaster of Paris about ½-inch thick. When hard, remove cardboard frame, wash plaster (outdoors) and paint with poster paint or water colours if desired.

If individual moulds are being made for a collection, make small circular or square moulds of approximately the same size to give the collection a pleasing appearance. Press a rock or shell into each while still wet and do not handle until set.

Seed Mosaic

On a square piece of cardboard draw a simple scene or a design, as in Fig. 98. Get a variety of any seeds from a pet shop or corn store, being sure they are packaged separately.

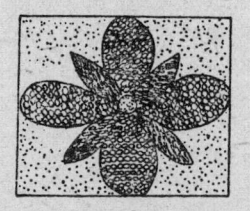

Fig. 98. Seed mosaic.

Only a handful is necessary of each kind: sunflower seed, barley, wheat, bird seed. Coat, with a layer of glue, all parts of the design to be covered with one type of seed. Arrange large seeds individually, or sprinkle small ones. When this is dry, repeat with another part of the design, and so on until it is covered.

HIKES AND FIELD TRIPS

A hike is a brisk walk, with walking the main point. A field trip means going slowly enough to see everything of special interest. On any field trip keep a sharp eye open for craft, decoration or collection items to bring home: seeds and cones, catkins and reeds, interesting branches and bark, rocks and moss.

Take any equipment that might be needed: a shoulder bag for finds, including small jars or cans with tight lids for water samples, lids with holes for insects or other animals, a notebook and pencil to record information, moulding equipment for track records (see "Nature Crafts"). The equipment will depend on your aims.

Marshlands and Ponds

Before investigating these, check for good footing to avoid bogs.

Since marshes and ponds are usually still water, they are particularly good sources for animal and plant study. Take home samples of scum and water to study under a microscope. Look for bird life in particular. Observe whether there are ducks, geese, herons or other water lovers such as coots and moorhens. Try to discover whether they are nesting or migrating; observe how they group themselves for flying.

Look for long reeds to bring home. The latter may be used for basket-making or mats.

The Farm

See what different animals are fed, where they are kept, how they care for their young. Why is the farmer raising them?

Observe the field crops. How are they planted, how cared for, when harvested? What will the product be used for (frozen foods, marketing, seed, canning, animal food)?

Find out which wild animals the farmer likes, which are pests. How does he care for the soil to prevent erosion and retain fertility?

Bring home dried weeds and seed pods for flower arrangements.

When visiting a farm, you will find that dawn and twilight are the most interesting times.

The River

Climb a hill to observe how a river flows: note the direction, the current as the river widens and narrows, the land surrounding it, the choppy sections and curves. Observe what the river does to its banks by studying trees, embankments, and other man-made protectors.

Walk along the bank and look for water and sand animals and plants, deadwood, erosion marks and tide marks. Watch for jumping fish. In the autumn keep a lookout in the shallow waters near the banks for schools of baby fish migrating after spawning. Watch insects alight on the water without breaking the surface tension.

Try to catch small river creatures — tadpoles, fish; fill a tub with river plants and water if possible and experiment with raising them. Feed them insects, bits of meat and lettuce, fish food.

If there is a waterfall, study what the force of the water is doing to the rocks above and below; discover why it is so powerful.

The Beach

The best time for a beach walk is at low tide. Tennis shoes are helpful for climbing around rocks. Local newspapers' tide tables can provide the time when an unusually low tide is expected. Things to look for: water and dune plants, water and sand animals and birds and the tracks they make, shifting sand, tide marks, the effect of water on rocks and pebbles. Small pools caught in the rocks when the tide goes out may contain a great deal of sea life, to be observed. Collect shells and driftwood and water-moulded glass. From a dune or hill observe colour changes in the water. Take care not to be cut off by rising tides.

Lakes

If possible observe from a hill. Try to discover why the water is there. Find the river or stream that feeds it, and one that carries its waters away.

Walk along the shore and look for animal tracks, wood, native plants and animals, trees that hug the water. Watch the wind create swells and whitecaps. Observe how small lagoons and inlets are protected. See the colour of the water change with the weather, the time of day, the depth of the water.

Try to discover reasons why the water is pure and clean, or murky and dirty. Test the water and try to discover reasons why it is warm or cold. Float sticks to test the current and, when you find a current, look for a reason why one should exist at that point.

Dams

If a dam is nearby, find out the reason for its existence: for safety, for water supply, hydroelectric or for irrigation.

If it is a large dam, walk across if permitted. Try to picture reasons why the engineers built it in that particular place, why that special height and thickness was necessary.

Some dams have fish ladders, like giant steps up the side, for fish going upstream to spawn (lay eggs). Discover how the ladders operate, and in autumn watch, if possible, as the fish jump them. See how specialised animals such as eels manage. In the spring watch for baby fish.

Mountains and Forests

These areas abound in trees, ferns, mosses and unusual rock formations to observe. Watch for native birds or glimpses of wild animals. Locate burrows, nests, tree holes of birds. Look under rocks, logs, or loose bark for insects. Study the life rings of a tree stump. Compare trees to discover the varieties of the same family, such as pine.

Where the ground is moist look for animal tracks. Dig up a bit of soil with a stick and see the layers of rich humus that the trees are giving to the earth.

See how rivers and streams and waterfalls change the face of the land. Study exposed rock formations that show how the soil was laid down in strata, layer by layer, then crushed into hard rock, and then perhaps tilted as the mountains were formed, aeons ago.

Make animal track moulds. Bring home rocks, cones, bark, twisted branches, leaves, feathers, for crafts, collections, or decoration.

Meadows and Fields

Unploughed fields and meadows are the best areas to look for wild grasses and flowers, for insects and small field animals such as mice and shrews. Observe ground-loving birds such as partridges and meadowlarks. Try to spot burrows and nests without disturbing them.

For a collection or "everlasting" arrangement, look for

dried grasses, thistles and seed stalks or flowers in abundance, pretty rocks or interesting twigs.

Around a City Block

Even if mountains, beach or country are inaccessible, there is a world of nature in your own back yard. Develop the habit of *seeing* what goes on around you: how the trees change with the seasons; how grass and weeds push up toward the light, even through the driveway asphalt; what wild animals such as birds and squirrels brave the presence of man in your neighbourhood.

Learn to ask questions: Why are certain types of plants grown so commonly in the area? Why do big trees crack the concrete around them? Why are flies drawn to the house?

One Aim

If there is a favourite spot near your home, or there is enough time at a farm or holiday area to cover the same trail more than once, specialise in what to observe. On one trip count the varieties of trees, get leaf samples, compare their bark and what uses they have. Perhaps you can discover the pests, or the flowers or birds that favour that environment. On other trips study and collect insects, or spend the time bird watching.

5

CONVALESCENCE

There are many suggestions given below to make convalescence a time of entertaining and worthwhile activity. A number of the ideas may be carried out alone by the convalescent, giving the family the opportunity to help when possible, without spoiling him by constant attention.

PRACTICAL HINTS

If the illness is contagious, use newspaper or paper bags for waste, gay paper plates, paper craft articles that can be burned. A large market bag can be hung on the edge of the mattress to catch scraps from play.

Bedside Table

If no table is available, use a card table or orange crate gaily covered. Keep necessaries handy: tissues, lotions, a damp washcloth in a dish to wipe hands during craft work. It is comforting to have a bell to call for assistance and a clock to keep track of time, plus a play clock for younger children set at a special time. ("When the clock hands reach here, Jimmy will be home.")

Simple Food Surprises

MILK SIPPERS: Occasionally use straws with gay faces. The convalescent can make one-inch discs of white paper or cardboard and draw his own faces, or flowers, or toys, then glue them to straws for himself and the other children.

CLOWN: Use a scoop of ice cream, a cone tipped on top for a hat, sweets for eyes and mouth, a doily on the plate as a ruff.

FLOWER SALAD: Place a rounded scoop of cottage cheese in the centre, surrounded by pineapple chunks as petals. Embed five or six raisins in the centre of the cottage cheese.

SUNSHINE SALAD: The same as the flower salad, omitting the raisins.

Visitors

If the convalescent is well enough and his illness is not contagious, he might have a small friend in for lunch or even dinner. Parents should watch the patient for signs of fatigue and permit only one or two visitors at a time.

When friends or relatives want to bring something or to help, a "sunshine box" might be suggested. This is a box of individually wrapped trinkets, to be opened, perhaps, at stated times.

Protector

Use soft plastic to cover bedclothes for messy craft work.

Back Rest

Pillows slip and tire the back. If convalescence is to be long, buy a beach back rest, or put a straight chair upside down under the mattress, the latter resting against the sloping chair back. Or use a board inclined against the headboard. Place a pillow under the knees.

Book Holder

Buy one, or make by bending a wire coat hanger and hanging it over a tray tilted against knees or pillow.

Toys

There should be many, all easily workable. They should be practical for bed play. Avoid messy types or those with small parts that may get lost. This is the time for the box of toys put away because they had grown too familiar, or the Christmas overflow. This is the time for the kaleidoscope, the viewer with coloured film transparencies, the blackboard and magic slate; for board games, especially those of pure chance that permit an imaginary opponent. Save old magazines, catalogues, cardboard and scraps of all kinds, for crafts and other play.

Shoe Bag

Pin one to the edge of the mattress or across the headboard to hold small, constantly used items.

Change of Scene

If not too ill or suffering from a contagious disease, the closer the convalescent is to the centre of things, the happier he will be.

Writing Board

Purchase at a stationers. Use for writing or to hold book or craft materials.

Activity Tray

To prevent small toys, pegs, etc., from getting lost in a game, make an activity tray. Get a medium-size carton with an uncut lid. Remove lid, cut the sides down to about three inches from the bottom, dipping to one inch on the side that will face the convalescent. Place the flat lid, smooth side up, in the bottom of the box. This permits play with miniature toys or other games that require flat, unbroken surfaces. The tray can then be removed as set up, for later play. A larger box can be used to make a flat surface for board games.

Entertainment

Members of the family should take turns carrying in trays to the convalescent, as well as running errands, reading and so on, for variety.

Make a "surprise ball" (see page 47) for the convalescent, and later have him make one for a friend.

The convalescent will enjoy things to watch: a dish

Convalescence

garden, a fish, a bird if patient is not allergic to it. A bed placed near a window permits bird watching. A bird feeder or birdhouse outside the window makes this easier.

Use string across a wall for pinning up craft articles, interesting pictures, maps. A bulletin board made of wallboard can hold get-well cards and other treasures. Make a flannel board (see page 156) for play. Use a card table for supplies of crafts and so on. Clear it each night, however, so that everything will seem new daily. Make a bed table of boards between chairs, or use a stiff cardboard box with knee space cut out. Cover with oilcloth. (A real bed table is worth buying or making if the illness is long.)

When there are several pieces of mail, deliver one at a time, at breakfast, lunchtime, etc.

Radio and TV: A bedside radio and/or tape deck is a great source of comfort, especially to an older convalescent who may wish to learn words to the songs his friends are singing. One or two carefully chosen TV shows spaced throughout the day will give something to anticipate.

Schoolwork

If the convalescent is able to work, the teacher will help with suggestions to keep up on his schoolwork, and there are workbooks for various age levels. Reference books such as an encyclopedia set are invaluable. He might learn to type: the hunt-and-peck system if under ten, copying hand-printed words, if very young. For an older convalescent a book can be borrowed from school or library that will teach the touch-typing system.

Even a very small child can profit from foreign language lessons from a foreign friend or neighbour, and foreign language records are available at some libraries.

PLAY IDEAS

Getting well is usually a quiet time, and the play ideas given below are for just such times.

Here also are some suggestions especially suitable for convalescent periods: work on collections or hobbies. Make decorations and crafts for a holiday coming up. Make scrapbooks or mobiles. Bring the family photograph albums up to date. The convalescent can write to friends; listen to radio or watch TV — not more than one or one-and-a-half hours a day; learn to sew, weave, knit, crochet, braid, or embroider (see Chapter 2 for instructions).

Felt Board

Buy a light-weight plywood board or wallboard from a timber shop, 18 by 24 inches, plus green felt or baize to cover, with two inches to spare all around (22 by 28 inches). Pull the cloth neatly over board and drawing pin behind.

The baize board may be used to tell picture stories (see "Build a Town" and "Story Illustrations" which follow). If pictures are too lightweight to stick to the felt board, cut strips of sandpaper and glue to the back of each, rough side out.

Build a Town

This is a continuing game. One day the convalescent might "build" a school building. He can go through magazines for pictures relating to school children, schoolrooms, playgrounds, books. Or he can draw his own pictures, which is more fun if he enjoys drawing. The pictures may be used to tell a story on a felt board, or pinned to a curtain, or made into a simple scrapbook. Another day he might build a hospital, with nurses and doctors and medicines and flowers and new babies. Other suggestions: a home, a supermarket, a toy shop, a farm.

Story Illustrations

Pictures may be cut from a magazine, or drawn by hand, to tell a story read in a book. Paste to a large sheet of craft paper, or use on a felt board.

MY OWN STORY: On a large sheet of paper, the convalescent

Convalescence

can draw the foods eaten at the day's meals, or the people he has seen, or games and activities of the day. Or he can draw the story of his life (below).

Biography

The convalescent can make a scrapbook telling the life story of a character he has made up, or a storybook character, or the story of a real person. Or he can make a picture autobiography of his own life.

For these, pictures may be drawn or found in magazines, of babies doing different things, of a child going to school, older boys or girls biking or playing, grown people working. The pictures tell the story — of bad boy Joe and what made him change, or of Nancy who wanted to be a nurse, or whatever else the author wishes or the pictures suggest.

Miss Fancy's Come to Call (or Here Comes Ringo, for boys)

The convalescent pretends that a visitor has arrived and carries on a conversation with him. A parent can play this while working within easy hearing range. The parent or a brother or sister can be a neighbour, a favourite football player, the Prime Minister, or anyone else desired.

Ways with Buttons

1. Sort them by colour or size, putting different colours in separate small boxes.

2. Use buttons as food in doll games, spooning out with a soup spoon.

3. Make a button collection; ask friends to save pretty ones.

4. Make a mosaic for a decoration.

5. String into a necklace by going through both holes of the button so that it lies flat. Lay buttons out in a line first to make a pleasing pattern.

6. Collect enough large buttons to sew to a band of elastic for a belt. Or use corduroy or felt, sewing small buttons on in a pattern, such as a circle, triangle, or star.

Calendars

WEATHER CALENDAR: Copy on craft paper the calendar of the present month, or use a spare calendar. Each day place a weather symbol to suit the day's weather: a sun, a cloud, umbrella or drops of rain. At the end of the month count the number of days for each, and list them. This gives an excellent picture of the local weather. For other weather observations, see "Weather", page 128.

PICTURE CALENDAR: On a large sheet (18 by 24 inches or larger) of newsprint or wrapping paper make a calendar of the present month. Use an almanac, the encyclopedia and lists of your own family and church special days, birthdays, etc., to find events for each date. Draw appropriate pictures and label.

Uses for Mail Order Catalogues

1. Pictures for games, such as "Build a Town", "Story Illustrations", and "Biography" (see "Play Ideas").

2. Doll play pictures, paper dolls, stand-up pictures (see page 38).

3. Models to help draw your own pictures.

The Scribble Machine

Make a "scribble machine" by folding two or three sheets

Fig. 99. Scribble machine.

of white paper in half and stapling or tying together like a book (Fig. 99). On each page have family members — even Baby — or friends, scribble a mark. The convalescent adds to the scribble to make a figure, as shown by the dotted lines.

Helpful Fun

The convalescent often has a wonderful chance to help with family chores when the illness is not contagious. Here are several possibilities:

1. Restring all the broken strands of beads. Sort costume jewellery.

2. Help with the cooking. String beans, shell peas, crack nuts, break bread for stuffing.

3. Have the family's drawers placed, one or two at a time, on a card table, and tidy them. Place small items in open boxes for greater neatness: socks, crayons and pencils, ribbons.

Imaginary Travel

1. Pin up a world map and one of the U.K. For this use a door, bulletin board, wallboard, or a string across the wall. The geographic areas can be looked up when mentioned in book or conversation: counties, cities, rivers, countries, oceans.

2. Make a scrapbook of other countries or the U.K.

3. Write to local travel agency offices for literature on special spots of interest. Plan make-believe trips there. Look up information in the encyclopedia.

4. Choose one country or county and draw a large map of the area on shelf paper, wrapping paper or a market bag cut open. Cut out pictures of the area chosen and glue to the proper location. Thus for Kent the choice might be Canterbury Cathedral, etc.

Imaginary Games

With a nurse's cap, a soldier hat or a cowboy sombrero, the convalescent can direct the activities of a hospital, a troop of men or a roundup. This can be completely imaginary, or small toys may be used.

For an imaginary train, see page 81.

Miniature Theatres

Cut a side and the top from a medium-sized carton. Paste magazine pictures on the wall and floor for decoration and scenery: curtains, rugs, flowers, sometimes even a whole room scene from a magazine will suit. Or follow instructions for doll's house walls and furniture (see page 64), or use toy furniture.

Use miniature dolls, men, cars, etc., on this page, and act out a story with them. Change voices for the different characters or use records for songs. Or the dolls can act out stories told on records. Or give a complete puppet show. Make the puppets, the theatre and scenery, as above; write several scripts so you can change to a new one from time to time.

Painting in Bed

Use poster paints or water colours, both washable. Place paints on a firm surface such as a card table. Cover the floor with oilcloth, plastic, rags or newspapers, and the bedclothes with plastic.

Whenever possible it is better, while in bed, to use paper and glue instead of paint, for covering drums for example.

Old Nosey

Draw a face in profile on cardboard, leaving it blank between eye and mouth, as in Fig. 100. Cut a fine chain, such as a cheap pendant chain, twice as long as the distance between eye and mouth. Pierce holes in drawing at eye and mouth; force chain ends through holes and tape to the back of the cardboard. Shake the picture, causing the chain to form many different noses.

Convalescence 161

Fig. 100. Old Nosey.

Clock

Mark a paper plate with the twelve numbers on the clock. Cut two arrows of different lengths from bright craft paper pasted on cardboard. Attach to the centre of the plate with a brass paper fastener. The movable hands can be used to tell time.

The paper clock will also help pass the time. Set the hands at the time of the next visit from someone, or the time of the next pill, or at the hour that a brother or sister gets home from school, and watch for the real clock to match the toy.

6

TRAVEL

At travel time activities are best that require no equipment at all, or very few easily handled and packed materials. Below are games, ideas and activities suited to the special needs of travel. Suggestions for camping and family excursions are also included.

WHAT TO TAKE

In addition to the sports equipment and clothes needed on arrival, keep wholesome snacks and thermos drinks on hand for the trip. Check the toy shelves carefully for easily handled games or activities that hold interest while taking little space.

Always pack a pad of paper, crayons, pencil, possibly even blunt scissors, glue or sellotape. A writing board is inexpensive and will slip under the front seat for storage. A deck of cards and special travel-size games such as peg chess or peg draughts will be welcome if time is spent in trains, motels or hotels. A good book or two is always a good idea, and libraries usually permit longer lending in such cases. Add a song book and one of game suggestions such as those below. A soft ball, skipping rope or other easily packed equipment for active play is often welcome when stopping for a while during the day.

Try to find room for any special hobby equipment that will make the trip more worthwhile, such as art materials, camera and film, or nature hobby supplies — materials to make plaster casts of woodland animals, for example (see

Chapter 4). Often a shoe box will hold all your needs.

Looking up on-the-spot references adds tremendously to the fun of travel, so take along nature identification booklets on rocks, trees, birds, flowers or other special interests. Take also a shoulder bag to hold specimens.

WHAT TO BRING BACK

If possible, bring back interesting things you see. Private fields may not be entered of course, and nature items often should not be disturbed, but in spite of this travelling offers wonderful opportunities to add to collections. Sometimes there are stray plants on the edge of a field, or sprays of grain ready to harvest. Look for rock specimens, oak apples or acorns from oak trees, for your collections. Keep an eye out for interesting pieces of wood, seed pods or rushes for flower arrangements; moss, bark or cones for future crafts.

For a pressed flower collection, the practice on open lands where picking is permitted at all is to take a flower only where there are ten of the same variety within a square yard. Even then only one or two should be picked, and pressed immediately, because wild flowers wilt very quickly.

Other hobbies that profit from travel are coin collections, post-card or travel picture scrapbooks, history and geography.

WHAT TO SEE

Look for those features while travelling:

1. First of all, don't miss national parks and monuments, which are spots of unusual beauty.

2. Parks, beaches, river or harbour tours, lakes, zoos.

3. Places of historic interest including great houses and gardens, and other National Trust properties.

4. Guided tours through industrial plants that are characteristic of the area.

5. Sections that retain an old or exotic atmosphere.

6. Check dates for special events.

GAMES TO PLAY IN THE CAR

Car Counting Games

NUMBER PLATES: See who can spot the largest number of plates ending or beginning with a particular letter. One point may be given for each.

CAR-BUZZ, or CAR-FIZZ-BUZZ: Play these games (see Idea Games later in this section) by counting the cars you meet going in the opposite direction.

SUBTRACTIONS: Count the cars you meet, but subtract one for every car you pass or are passed by. For a very complicated game, play "Subtractions" and "Fizz-Buzz" (see Idea Games later in this section) at the same time.

NUMBER PLATE BINGO: Every time the chosen letter is seen, the first to spot it says "Bingo". Or, choose any number the players wish, such as number 4 and then every time a 4 is seen, call "Bingo". This can be combined with the letter. Thus if "W" and "4" were chosen, then HWL 242 W would rate "bingo, bingo, bingo".

Variation: A pencil record may be kept if desired. If this is done mark one column with the letter, one column by the number you are "collecting". Game is won by the first player to get ten in *each* column.

Observation Games

TRAVEL I SPY: One player is chosen to name something that all must watch for: a white horse or a red barn or a hitch-hiker. The first one to see the object calls, "I spy" and then may choose the next object. If he chooses *white horse*, for example, and none is seen for some time, another player may call "Time" and he must choose another object.

TRAVEL ABC: This is a type of "I spy". Players look for letters of the alphabet in commercial signs, road signs, and elsewhere. The letters must be found in order. Smaller children can look together for the letters; older children can compete. If someone sees an "a" in "Apple Valley", he can claim the first "a", but if his opponent is quick, he will see the "a" in "Valley", too, and be able to claim one also.

ANIMAL FARM: Each player collects animals for his farm. The first to see a tiger on a sign, for example, or a sheep in a pasture, has that animal in his farm. At the end of a specified time the one with the most animals wins.

Variation: Each player draws his animals on paper as he sees them. Printed names may be added, as in a zoo.

MAP GAMES:

1. Draw a map while travelling, marking in what is seen. Have a sheet of paper for each hundred miles to be travelled. For map symbols to use, see page 145 or make up your own. Make a key in the corner to identify the symbols.

2. Follow the road map while riding in the car, learning what the symbols are, learning to read distances, looking for special points of interest.

Idea Games

THREE WORDS: Players take turns. Each chooses any three words he can think of and calls upon another player to make a sentence of them. Thus *mountains, box, rope,* may be used to say, "I carried a box lunch with a rope, and ate it when I reached the mountains".

BUZZ (nine years and up): Take turns counting. Player

number 1 saying "One", next player, "Two", and on up. Every time a seven or a multiple of seven is used, say "Buzz" instead: 1-2-3-4-5-6-*buzz*-8-9 . . . 13-*buzz*-15 . . . The seventies would be *buzz*-1, buzz-2 . . . *buzz*-6, *buzz-buzz*.

BUZZ, JR. (six to eight years): Played as "Buzz" above, but "Buzz" is used in place of 10: 1-2-3-4-5-6-7-8-9-*buzz* . . .

FIZZ-BUZZ (nine years and up): Played as "Buzz", above, except that when 5 or a multiple is used, *fizz* is said instead: when 7 or a multiple of 7 is used, *buzz* is said. Those who miss drop out. Example: 1-2-3-4-*fizz*-6-*buzz*-8-9-*fizz*-11-12-13-*buzz*-*fizz*-16.

FIZZ-BUZZ, JR. (six to eight years): The same as "Buzz, Jr.", except that 5 and 10 and their multiples are replaced: 1-2-3-4-*fizz*-6-7-8-9-*buzz*-11 . . .

DESCRIPTION: Players take turns describing any object they choose, using as many descriptive adjectives as they can think of: "The alligator is huge, horrid and hideous." "The brown-eyed Susan is pretty, fragrant and yellow." Younger players might say instead, "The brown-eyed Susan has a lot of petals and is like the sun", for the purpose of the game is to describe an object in as many ways as possible.

Variation: This can be played as a guessing game by saying "I'm thinking of an animal that is huge, horrid and hideous." Other hints may be given as needed.

TWENTY QUESTIONS: Players take turns thinking of an object that is animal (live, or a product of a live animal, such as milk); vegetable (plant or product of a plant such as cotton); or mineral. Other players must guess in twenty questions or less. All answers must be "yes" or "no".

COFFEEPOT (six years and up): Played somewhat like "Twenty Questions", above, except that the word sought is always a verb — doing something. When others ask questions to discover what verb you are thinking of, all must use the word "coffeepot" as a substitute for the verb. Here

Travel 167

is a simplified example of how the game is played: "Does everybody coffeepot?" "Yes." "Do they coffeepot at mealtimes?" "Yes." "Is it *eat*?" "No." "Drink?" "Yes."

TEAKETTLE (eight years and up): This is a game of *homonyms* (homo-nims), words that sound alike but mean something different. Substitute the word "teakettle" for the homonyms in a sentence, and the other players must guess the word in mind:

Example: "The *teakettle teakettled* the shepherd and was soothed." (... herd heard ...) "The *teakettle* was one of a *teakettle* hanging from the tree; Mother will *teakettle* it." (... pear ... pair ... pare ...)

Here are several other homonyms: bear, bare; dear, deer; shoe, shoo; stair, stare; no, know; read, reed; here, hear; there, their; reel, real; sort, sought; berry, bury.

Variation: Each player may write a sentence containing *teakettle* words, and then read it aloud when time is called, for other players to guess.

A QUARTER OF A GHOST (ten years and up): One player begins by giving a letter of the alphabet. The next player adds a letter. It must not spell a finished word, but he must have a word in mind. Thus, if the first letter is *a* he might add *p*, thinking of *apple*. Each player adds a letter being careful not to spell a word. If he spells a word, or can think of no letter to add on, he is a quarter of a ghost. Thus the third player may add *t*, spelling apt, and become a quarter of a ghost. If he insteads adds *p* he is safe — for the moment. If he can think of no letter he or anyone else may challenge the previous player who, if he had no word in mind, is then a quarter of a ghost. Each player is permitted three misses, until he is three quarters of a ghost. On the fourth miss he is out. The winner is the last one in the game.

ASSOCIATION (six years and up): The one who is "It" says five words, and each player writes, or says aloud, the first word he thinks of when he hears each. If written, answers are read aloud later.

Variation: Players take turns calling a player's name, and then saying a word. The one called must instantly say what it makes him think of.

CATEGORIES (nine years and up): Choose some particular group of objects you wish to name. It can be a geographic group as cities, mountains, rivers. It can be boys' or girls' names, animals, trees, flowers, or anything else desired.

Each player has a pencil and a large sheet of paper on which he writes the alphabet, leaving space for five or six names under or opposite each letter. Then, at a signal, the players attempt to write as many of the chosen group as they can think of under each letter. Give one point for each name, plus twenty-five points for a complete list — that is, at least one name under each letter. Call time when it is obvious that the players are running out of names or growing restive.

Variation (six years and up): The player who is "It" chooses a category, such as animals, or boys' names that begin with *B*, or any other choice. All players take turns adding to the list. Those who cannot add a word on three tries drop out. Or all players may make lists on paper and compare results when time is called. For younger players the game should be oral, or a written score may be kept by an adult.

IMAGINATION: This is a guessing game. "Where am I?" the one who is "It" asks. Other players begin to guess. The answers must be "yes" or "no", but if other players cannot locate "where", "It" may direct them with "warm", "hot", "red hot", "cold", "freezing", etc., since "It" may be in a place so small the others don't think of it at all — sitting on the horn, or behind the rear-view mirror, or in a trouser cuff.

EXCURSIONS

In a file keep a list of interesting places to see. Of course the list will be headed with the nearest zoo, museum and playgrounds. When friends recount local trips, write them down for a future visit by the family.

The newspaper is another source of interesting excursions. It will list theatres, sports events, fairs, and special shows such as hobby, craft or Scout exhibits. It will report on what to see at particular times in public gardens or planetariums.

In addition to these, there may be an aquarium, a domestic animal farm, art centres, commercial fun spots or piers nearby. You may live near an Army installation, the home of a famous person, a university, castle or battleground. Some of the historic houses in your section may be open to the public. Jot these down, together with address and opening days or hours when possible.

Do not forget places of business that sometimes permit visitors or conduct tours; car assembly plants, the post office, a newspaper office, the telephone and water supply companies, a bakery. The fruit, vegetable, flower and meat markets in the morning hours, canneries and nurseries, harbours and commercial fishing wharves, and many more industrial areas are fascinating spots to visit with the family.

CAMPING

Any holiday is fun, but many young people enjoy camping perhaps most of all. Often one year's holiday budget comes close to paying for the camping equipment that will serve for many years, and all items can be rented.

Cooking Suggestions

Menu: Layered potato, baked apple or baked banana, milk or chocolate.

LAYERED POTATO: For each person take one baking potato, one cooking onion, one carrot, $\frac{1}{4}$ pound hamburger. Slice the unpeeled potato into three horizontal sections. Cut a one-foot square of heavy foil, or two one-foot squares of light foil. In this foil place the bottom layer of potato, a slice of onion, two slices of carrot side by side, a layer of half of the hamburger; then another layer of potato, onion, carrots, hamburger; and the top layer of potato. Wrap in foil and bake in coals for one hour. This can be prepared at home, wrapped tightly at once and taken ready to bake.

BAKED APPLE: Cut out the core of the apple, being careful not to go through the bottom skin. Fill with honey or brown sugar, wrap in foil, bake one half hour in coals. If prepared ahead of time at home, seal the top of the hole with butter. Apples can be baked as they are, uncored, and will be even more wholesome.

BAKED BANANA: Cut a peeled banana almost through in one-inch slices. Into each slit insert a miniature marshmallow or slice of a marshmallow and one square of a small chocolate bar. Seal with foil. Bake in coals for fifteen minutes.

Index

A

Absorption of water, 121
Accessories box, 52
Activity tray, 154
Aeroplanes as a hobby, 89
African native hut, 82
American Indian war canoe, 73
Animal farm, 165
    tracks, 143
Animals, 131
Aquarium, 132
Archaeology, 96
Art as a hobby, 89
"Association", 167
Astronomy, 112

B

Baked apple, 170
    banana, 170
Basket bag, 50
Beach combing, 149
Beads, 29, 30, 31
Bedside table, 152
Biography, 157
Birds, 132
    eggs, 133
    nests, 133
Book ends, 53
    holder, 153
    rest, 153
Booklet boxes, 14
Books, 10
Border prints, 20
Bottle-cap boat, 75
Box cars, 82
    designs, 19
Bracelet, 29
Braided rug, 91
Braiding, 90
Butterflies, 135
Button games, 157
    mosaics, 29
"Buzz", 165

C

Calendars, 158
Camping, 169
Candle holder, 16
Car games, 164
Cardboard clock, 161
Carnation, 31
Carpentry supplies, 12
Cars and trucks as a hobby, 91
Carton doll's house, 62
"Categories", 168
Catharine wheel flowers, 34
Chemistry, 120
Clay, 15
"Clown", 153
"Coffeepot", 166
Coil bowl, 16
Coins as a hobby, 91
Collage, 25
Collecting, 87
Colour tricks, 116
Coloured carnations, 32
    top, 116
Conduction of heat, 120
Convalescence, 152 et seq.

Cooking as a hobby, 92
    suggestions for camping, 169
Cotton modelling (animals), 18
    reel beads, 31
Cow hitch, 97
"Craft" paper, 12
Craft plan, 11
    razor, 13
    supplies, 12
    work, 88
Crayon and paints designs, 27
    on cloth, 26
    —scratch designs, 27
Crêpe paper flowers, 33
Crime detection, 121
Crossed wire mobile, 39
Cushions, 101
Cutout pictures, 25
Cut-paper designs, 24
Cutting circles, 11

D

Dams, 150
Decorated bottles, 44
    containers, 46
    picture frames, 37
    stationery, 49
Decorative birds, 40
"Description", 166
Diorama, 141
Doily picture frame, 37
Doll's house bed, 64
    bookcases, 66
    chairs, 67
    chest of drawers, 65
    coffee table, 66
    couch, 66
    cradle, 65
    curtains, 67
    decorations, 68 et seq.
    dining table, 66
    egg shell cradle, 65
    furniture, 64 et seq.
    lamps, 68
    lanterns, 70
    linoleum floor, 63
    mirrors, 68
    mobile, 70
    pictures, 68
    pillows, 66
    plants and trees, 68
    rugs, 69
    side tables, 65
    studio couch, 65
    table centre-piece, 68
    wallpaper, 63
Door stop, 52

E

Earrings, 29
Earthworms, 140
Elf bag, 100
Enclosures, 84
Engine, 81
Excursions, 168

F

Farms, 148
Felt board, 156

Fences, 84
Field trips, 147
Fields, 150
Fish, 148
    ladders, 150
"Fizz-buzz", 166
Flat waggons, 82
Flower arranging, 92
    salad, 153
    tree, 35
Foil doll, 71
Folding cardboard, 11
Forests, 150
Free form wax designs, 43

G

Gardening, 94 *et seq.*
    experiments, 95
Geography, 96, 123
Geology, 124
Glue, types of, 11
Goods trucks, 82
Grocery carton separators, 83

H

Hand print, 17
Hanging a mobile, 40
Heat experiments, 119, 120
Helicopter, 79, 80
Helpfulness, 159
Hikes, 147
History, 96
Home decorating, 97

I

Imaginary games, 160
    travel, 160
"Imagination", 168
Indoor gardening, 94
Ink prints, 146
Insects, 134

J

"Jewelled" box, 51

K

Knot tying, 97

L

Lakes, 149
Large sheets of paper, 11
Laundry bag doll, 105
Layered potato, 169
Leaf collection, 137
    prints, 137 *et seq.*
Leather thongs, 98
    work, 98
Litter bag, 53
Log cabins, model, 85

M

Mail order catalogues, 158
Map games, 165
    making, 145
Marbelized paper, 27

Marshlands, 148
Matchbox trains, 82
Meadows, 150
Milk sippers, 152
Miniature bathroom appliances, 62
    bed, 59
    bedspread, 59
    bench, 61
    blankets, 59
    bookcases, 61
    carnation, 32
    chairs, 61
    chests, 62
    coffee table, 61
    curtains, 61
    dishes, 61
    dressing table, 62
    kitchen appliances, 62
    mattress, 59
    pillow, 59
    settee, 59
    sheets, 59
    side tables, 61
    tables, 61
    theatres, 160
Mobiles, 38 *et seq.*
Model tent, 78
Mosaics, 27
Moulded bowl, 15
Mountains, 150

N

Nature, 131 *et seq.*
    in the city, 151
    jewellery, 145
Number plate bingo, 164
    game, 164

O

Obligation to amuse children, 9
Old nosey, 160
Optical illusion, 115
Ornamental cotton reel doll, 71

P

Painting in bed, 160
Paper boat, 73
    house, 53
    tent, 54
    trees, 69
Papier maché, 15
Paste, 15
    board, 12
Patterns, 13
Pen-wipers, 49
Pencil holders, 45
Perspective, 124
Petal flowers, 31
Pets, 98
Photography, 98, 99
Physics, 126
Physiology, 115
Picture calendar, 158
    frames, 36
    stand, 37
Piggy bank, home-made, 77
Pipe cleaner dolls, 70
Plaster of Paris, 15, 146
    casts of tracks, 143
Plastic purse envelope, 52

Index

Pompoms, 73
Ponds, 148
Prehistoric times, 99
Punch-dot mosaics, 28

Q

"Quarter of a ghost", 167
Quilting, 103

R

Rain gauge, 129
Rainbow, 116
Reed basket 145
Reference file, 13
    folder, 13
Repeating designs, 20
Research, 88
Rivers, 148
Road safety, 127
Rock pools, 149
Rocks, 135

S

Sardine can shadow box, 143
School work for convalescent, 155
Science, 112 et seq.
Scrap-book, 88
Scribble machine, 158
Seaside hobbies, 136
Seed collection, 138
    mosaic, 147
Sewing, 99
    box, 50
    stitches, 103
    supplies, 12
Shadow boxes, 142
Shell scene, 25
Shells, 136
Ships as a hobby, 107
Shoe bag, 154
    box barn, 58
        church, 56
        grocery shop, 57
        house, 55
            furnishings, 59
        inn, 56
        ranch style house, 57
        suitcase, 76
        village, 55
Simplified doll's house, 64
Snowflake designs, 22
Soap carving, 17
Sock doll, 71
Soil conservation, 127
Sound, 117
Sponge animals, 19
Stained-glass medallions, 42
Stamp collecting, 107
Stand-up animals, 78
        pictures, 38
Stargazers, 114

Stencils, 20
Stone walls, 84
Stones, 135
Story pictures, 156
Stretcher, 79
Sunshine box, 153
    salad, 153
Surprise ball, 47

T

Tadpoles, 140
Tanker waggon, 82
Tassels, 73
Taste, 117
"Teakettle", 167
Terrarium, 144
Textured crayon pictures, 26
    painting, 26
"Three words", 165
Thunder and lightning, 117
Tie, 100
Tile mosaic, 27
Torn-paper designs, 24
Touch, 118
Toys in convalescence, 153
Traditional circus waggon, 75
Train of boxes, 81
Trains as a hobby, 108
Travel ABC, 165
    I-spy, 164
    shoe bag, 106
    time activities, 162 et seq.
Trees, 137
Triangle mobile, 39
Tulips, 34
"Twenty questions", 166
Twig identification, 139

V

Vase, 46

W

Wall bowl of fruit, 43
Wallet, 80
Wallpaper ideas, 23
Walnut boat, 74
Wax designs, free form, 43
Weather, 128
Weaving, 108
Whittling, 110
Wild flowers, 134
    pets, 140
Wire clothes hanger mobile, 39
Wood collection, 139
Woven belt, 110
    paper, 22
    mats, 22
    purse, 108
Writing, 111
    board, 154
    supplies, 12

Other **paperfronts**

CHILDREN'S PARTY
AND
GAMES BOOK

By Joyce Nicholson

There's no need to worry about giving a kiddies' party.

Starting with planning the party and sending out invitations the book goes on to deal with over 100 games.

Includes energetic and quiet games, musical games, pencil and paper games and races.

Also offers suggestions for themes for special parties, e.g. pirate parties and fairy parties.

128 value-packed pages

Uniform with this book

ELLIOT RIGHT WAY BOOKS, KINGSWOOD, SURREY, U.K.

BEGIN CHESS

By David Pritchard

Begin Chess is simple enough to be understood by children. It is clear, authoritative—and revolutionary. No insight is needed to understand why it has been acclaimed as a classic, and published all over the English-speaking world.

David Pritchard is one of Britain's top-graded players, and holder of many titles. His other book, "The Right Way To Play Chess" (a **paperfront**), was first published 27 years ago, and remains a bestseller. It has been widely applauded.

160 value-packed pages

Uniform with this book

ELLIOT RIGHT WAY BOOKS, KINGSWOOD, SURREY, U.K.

OUR PUBLISHING POLICY

HOW WE CHOOSE

Our policy is to consider every deserving manuscript and we can give special editorial help where an author is an authority on his subject but an inexperienced writer. We are rigorously selective in the choice of books we publish. We set the highest standards of editorial quality and accuracy. This means that a *Paperfront* is easy to understand and delightful to read. Where illustrations are necessary to convey points of detail, these are drawn up by a subject specialist artist from our panel.

HOW WE KEEP PRICES LOW

We aim for the big seller. This enables us to order enormous print runs and achieve the lowest price for you. Unfortunately, this means that you will not find in the *Paperfront* list any titles on obscure subjects of minority interest only. These could not be printed in large enough quantities to be sold for the low price at which we offer this series.

We sell almost all our *Paperfronts* at the same unit price. This saves a lot of fiddling about in our clerical departments and helps us to give you world-beating value. Under this system, the longer titles are offered at a price which we believe to be unmatched by any publisher in the world.

OUR DISTRIBUTION SYSTEM

Because of the competitive price, and the rapid turnover, *Paperfronts* are possibly the most profitable line a bookseller can handle. They are stocked by the best bookshops all over the world. It may be that your bookseller has run out of stock of a particular title. If so, he can order more from us at any time — we have a fine reputation for "same day" despatch, and we supply any order, however small (even a single copy), to any bookseller who has an account with us. We prefer you to buy from your bookseller, as this reminds him of the strong underlying public demand for *Paperfronts*. Members of the public who live in remote places, or who are housebound, or whose local bookseller is unco-operative, can order direct from us by post.

FREE

If you would like an up-to-date list of all paperfront titles currently available, send a stamped self-addressed envelope to
ELLIOT RIGHT WAY BOOKS, BRIGHTON RD.,
LOWER KINGSWOOD, SURREY, U.K.